SURVIVING AI

COMMENTS ON *SURVIVING AI*

A sober and easy-to-read review of the risks and opportunities that humanity will face from AI.

Jaan Tallinn,
co-founder *Skype*, co-founder *Centre for the Study of Existential Risk (CSER)*, co-founder *Future of Life Institute (FLI)*

Understanding AI – its promise and its dangers – is emerging as one of the great challenges of coming decades and this is an invaluable guide to anyone who's interested, confused, excited or scared.

David Shukman,
BBC Science Editor

As artificial intelligence drives the pace of automation ever faster, it is timely that we consider in detail how it might eventually make an even more profound change to our lives – how truly general AI might vastly exceed our capabilities in all areas of endeavour. The opportunities and challenges of this scenario are daunting for humanity to contemplate, let alone to manage in our best interests. We have recently seen a surge in the volume of scholarly analysis of this topic; Chace impressively augments that with this high-quality, more general-audience discussion.

Aubrey de Grey,
CSO, *SENS Research Foundation,*
and former AI researcher

Calum Chace provides a clear, simple, stimulating summary of the key positions and ideas regarding the future of Artificial General Intelligence and its potential risks. For the newcomer who's after a non-technical, even-handed intro to the various perspectives being bandied about regarding these very controversial issues, Chace's book provides a great starting-point into the literature.

It's rare to see a book about the potential End of the World that is fun to read without descending into sensationalism or crass oversimplification.

Ben Goertzel,
chairman, *Novamente LLC*

Calum Chace is a prescient messenger of the risks and rewards of artificial intelligence. In *Surviving AI* he has identified the most essential issues and developed them with insight and wit – so that the very framing of the questions aids our search for answers. Chace's sensible balance between AI's promise and peril makes *Surviving AI* an excellent primer for anyone interested in what's happening, how we got here, and where we are headed.

Surviving AI remains clear and jargon-free, enabling newcomers to the subject to understand why many of today's most prominent thinkers have felt compelled to speak out publicly about it.

David Wood,
chair, *London Futurists*

Artificial intelligence is the most important technology of our era. Technological unemployment could force us to adopt an entirely new economic structure, and the creation of superintelligence would be the biggest event in human history. *Surviving AI* is a first-class introduction to all of this.

Brad Feld,
co-founder *Techstars*

The promises and perils of machine superintelligence are much debated nowadays. But between the complex and sometimes esoteric writings of AI theorists and academics like Nick Bostrom, and the popular-press prognostications of Elon Musk, Bill Gates and Stephen Hawking, there is something of a gap. Calum Chace's *Surviving AI* bridges that gap perfectly. It provides a compact yet rigorous guide to all the major arguments and issues in the field. An excellent resource for those who are new to this topic.

John Danaher,
Institute for Ethics and Emerging
Technologies (IEET)

Calum Chace strikes a note of clarity and balance in

the important and often divisive dialogue around the benefits and potential dangers of artificial intelligence. It's a debate we need to have, and Calum is an accessible and helpful guide.

Ben Medlock,
co-founder *Swiftkey*

The appearance of Calum Chace's book is of some considerable personal satisfaction to me, because it signifies the fact that the level of social awareness of the rise of massively intelligent machines (that I call artilects = artificial intellects) has finally reached the "third phase" i.e. what I call "mainstream" (phase zero = no awareness, phase one = intellectuals crying in the wilderness, phase two = action groups, phase three = mainstream, phase four = politics). As one of the tiny handful of people in the 80s in phase one, it has been a lonely business, so with Chace's book explaining what I call "the species dominance debate" to a mass audience, it is clear that humanity is now well into phase three.

The down-to-earth clarity of Chace's style will help take humanity into what could be a very violent, "Transcendence" movie-like, real-life, phase four. If you want to survive this coming fourth phase in the next few decades and prepare for it, you cannot afford NOT to read Chace's book.

Prof. Dr. Hugo de Garis,
author of *The Artilect War*, former director of the
Artificial Brain Lab, Xiamen University, China.

Advances in AI are set to affect progress in all other areas in the coming decades. If this momentum leads to the achievement of strong AI within the century, then in the words of one field leader it would be "the biggest event in human history". Now is therefore a perfect time for the thoughtful discussion of challenges and opportunities that Chace provides.

Surviving AI is an exceptionally clear, well-researched and balanced introduction to a complex and controversial topic, and is a compelling read to boot.

Seán Ó hÉigeartaigh,
executive director, *Cambridge Centre for the Study of Existential Risk*

CALUM writes fiction and non-fiction, primarily on the subject of artificial intelligence. In March 2015 he published *Pandora's Brain*, a techno-thriller about the arrival of the first conscious machine. He is a regular speaker on artificial intelligence and related technologies and runs a blog on the subject at www.pandoras-brain.com.

Prior to writing *Pandora's Brain*, Calum had a 30-year career in journalism and business, in which he was a marketer, a strategy consultant and a CEO. He maintains his interest in business by serving as chairman and coach for a selection of growing companies. In 2000 he co-wrote *The Internet Startup Bible*, a business best-seller published by Random House (now Penguin Random House).

He studied philosophy at Oxford University, where he discovered that the science fiction he had been reading since early boyhood is actually philosophy in fancy dress.

Also by Calum Chace

Pandora's Brain

The Internet Startup Bible (co-authored)

SURVIVING AI
CALUM CHACE

Three Cs Publishing

For Julia and Alex

SURVIVING AI

A Three Cs book.

ISBN: 978-0-9932116-2-1

First Published in 2015 by Three Cs.

Copyright © Calum Chace 2015

Cover and interior design © Rachel Lawston at
Lawston Design, www.lawstondesign.com

Photography © iStockphoto.com

The right of Calum Chace to be identified as the author
of this work has been asserted by him in accordance
with the Copyright, Design and Patents Act 1988

Printed and bound by CreateSpace

CONTENTS

INTRODUCTION
SURVIVING AI

Artificial intelligence (AI) is humanity's most powerful technology. Software that solves problems and turns data into insight is transforming our lives at an accelerating pace.

For most of us, the most obvious manifestation of AI today are our smartphones. We take them for granted now, but many of us are glued to them: they bring all the world's knowledge to our fingertips, as well as angry birds and zombies.

They are emphatically not just a luxury for people in developed countries: they provide clever payment systems, education, and market information which enable people in the emerging markets to compete and participate in the modern world.

The evolution of smartphones so far offers an intriguing analogy for the development of AI in the future. Nobody suggested thirty years ago that we would have powerful AIs in our pockets in the form of telephones, but now that it has happened it seems obvious. It is also entirely logical. We are highly social animals. Because we have language we can communicate complicated ideas, suggestions and instructions; we can work together in large teams and organise, produce economic surpluses, develop technologies. It's because of our unrivalled ability to communicate that we control the fate of this planet and every species on it.

It wasn't and couldn't have been predicted in advance, but in hindsight what could be more logical than our most powerful technology, AI, becoming available to most of us in the form of a communication device?

Thirty years ago we didn't know how the mobile phone market would develop. Today we don't know how the digital disruption which is transforming so many industries will evolve over the next thirty years. We don't know whether technological unemployment will be the result of the automation of jobs by AI, or whether humans will find new jobs in the way we have done since the start of the industrial revolution. What is the equivalent of the smartphone phenomenon for digital disruption and automation? Chances are it will be something different from what most people expect today, but it will look entirely natural and predictable in hindsight.

Making forecasts is risky, especially about the future, but the argument of this book is that AI will present a series of formidable challenges alongside its enormous benefits; that we should monitor the changes that are happening, and adopt policies which will encourage the best possible outcomes. The range of possible outcomes is wide, from the terrible to the wonderful, and they are not pre-determined. They will be selected partly by luck, partly by their own internal logic, but partly also by the policies embraced at all levels of society.

Individuals must prepare themselves to be as flexible as possible to meet the challenges of a fast-changing world. Organisations must try and anticipate the changes most relevant to them, and adapt their strategies and tactics accordingly. Governments must frame regulations which will encourage the better outcomes and fend off the worst ones. To some extent they must deploy the huge financial and human resources at their disposal too, although given the uncertainty about future developments which will prevail at all stages, they must be cautious about this.

Automation and superintelligence are the two forces which we can already see are likely to cause huge impacts. Many people remain sceptical about them, and other forces may emerge in the coming decades. Nevertheless they are the main focus of this book.

Automation could lead to an economic singularity. "Singularity" is a term borrowed from maths and physics, and means a point where the normal rules cease to apply, and what lies beyond is un-knowable to anyone this side of the event horizon.[1] An economic singularity might lead to an elite owning the means of production and suppressing the rest of us in a dystopian

(1) The term economic singularity was first used (as far as I can tell) by the economist Robin Hanson: http://mason.gmu.edu/~rhanson/fastgrow.html

technological authoritarian regime. Or it could lead to an economy of radical abundance, where nobody has to work for a living, and we are all free to have fun, and stretch our minds and develop our faculties to the full. I hope and believe that the latter is possible, but we also need to make sure the process of getting there is as smooth as possible.

The arrival of superintelligence, if and when it happens, would represent a technological singularity (usually just referred to as "the singularity"), and would be the most significant event in human history, bar none. Working out how to survive it is the most important challenge facing humanity in this and the next generation(s).

If we avoid the pitfalls, it will improve life in ways which are quite literally beyond our imagination. A superintelligence which recursively improved its own architecture and expanded its capabilities could very plausibly solve almost any human problem you can think of. Death could become optional and we could enjoy lives of constant bliss and excitement. If we get it wrong it could spell extinction. Because of the enormity of that risk, the majority of this book addresses superintelligence: the likelihood of it arriving, and of it being beneficial.

*

Surviving AI is a companion book to *Pandora's Brain*, a techno-thriller about the arrival of the first superintelligence. Further information about the ideas explored in both books is available at www.pandoras-brain.com.

PART ONE: ANI

Artificial Narrow Intelligence

CHAPTER 1
ARTIFICIAL INTELLIGENCE IN THE PAST AND THE PRESENT

1.1 – Definitions

Intelligence

Artificial intelligence (AI) is intelligence demonstrated by a machine or by software. But that statement doesn't take us very far: we're going to have to dig into both halves of it.

Intelligence, like most words used to describe what the brain does, is hard to pin down: there are many rival definitions. Most of them contain the notion of the ability to acquire information, and use it to achieve a goal. One of the most popular recent definitions is from German academic Marcus Hutter and Shane Legg, a co-founder of a company called DeepMind that we will hear about later. It states that "intelligence measures an agent's general ability to achieve goals in a wide range of environments." [2]

As well as being hard to define, intelligence is also hard to measure. There are many types of information that an intelligent being might want to acquire, and many types of goals it might want to achieve.

An American psychologist called Howard Gardner has distinguished nine types of intelligence: linguistic, logic-mathematical, musical, spatial, bodily, interpersonal, intrapersonal, existential and naturalistic. [3] Just listing them is sufficient for our purposes: we don't need to examine each one. Gardner has been criticised for not providing experimental evidence for these categories, but teachers and thinkers find them very useful.

Certainly, we all know that people vary in the type of intelligence they possess. Some are good at acquiring dry factual knowledge such as the birth dates of kings and queens, yet hopeless at using their knowledge to achieve goals, like making new friends. Others struggle to learn things from books or lessons, but are quick to understand what other people want, and hence become very popular.

When thinking about intelligence, a host of associated notions crowd in, such as reasoning, memory, understanding, learning and planning.

Machine

The second half of the definition of artificial intelligence specified that the intelligence has to be demonstrated by

(2) http://arxiv.org/pdf/0712.3329v1.pdf

(3) http://skyview.vansd.org/lschmidt/Projects/The%20Nine%20Types%20of%20Intelligence.html

a machine, or by software. The machine in question is usually a computer, although it could be any device created by humans – or indeed by an alien species. Today's computers use processors made of silicon, but in future other materials like graphene may come into play.

("Computer" is an old word which pre-dates the invention of electronic machines by several centuries. Originally it meant a person who calculates, and in the early twentieth century companies employed thousands of clerks to spend long and tedious days doing jobs which today's pocket calculators could do in moments.)

Software is a set of instructions that tell electronic signals how to dance together inside a machine. Whether intelligence resides in the machine or in the software is analogous to the question of whether it resides in the neurons in your brain or in the electrochemical signals that they transmit and receive. Fortunately we don't need to answer that question here.

ANI and AGI

We do need to discriminate between two very different types of artificial intelligence: artificial narrow intelligence (ANI) and artificial general intelligence (AGI[4]), which are also known as weak AI and strong AI, and as ordinary AI and full AI.

The easiest way to do this is to say that artificial general intelligence, or AGI, is an AI which can carry

(4) The term AGI has been popularised by AI researcher Ben Goertzel, although he gives credit for its invention to Shane Legg and others: http://wp.goertzel.org/who-coined-the-term-agi/

out any cognitive function that a human can. We have long had computers which can add up much better than any human, and computers which can play chess better than the best human chess grandmaster. However, no computer can yet beat humans at every intellectual endeavour.

The important distinction between narrow AI and AGI is about more than successful competition across a wide range of domains. It involves goal-setting. Ordinary AI simply does what we tell it to. An AGI will have has the ability to reflect on its goals and decide whether to adjust them. It will have volition.

Some people (including me) think that probably means an AGI will need to have self-awareness and be conscious, but this is a hunch rather than a proposition that can be proved yet.

Finally, some people prefer the term "machine intelligence" to AGI. Quite reasonably, they point out that we don't call airplanes "artificial aviation" to distinguish them from birds. But AGI seems to have become the standard usage, and it is a natural opposite to narrow AI. If and when the first AGI is created, it will no doubt choose an entirely new name for itself.

1.2 – A short history of AI research

Durable myths

Stories about artificially intelligent creatures go back at least as far as the ancient Greeks. Hephaestus (Vulcan to the Romans) was the blacksmith of Olympus: as well as creating Pandora, the first woman, he created life-like metal automatons.

More recently, science fiction got started with Mary Shelley's *Frankenstein* in the early nineteenth century, and in the early twentieth century Karel Capek's play *RUR* (Rossum's Universal Robots) introduced the idea of an uprising in which robots eliminate their human creators.

Alan Turing

The brilliant British mathematician and code-breaker Alan Turing is often described as the father of both computer science and artificial intelligence. His most famous achievement was breaking the German naval ciphers at the code-breaking centre at Bletchley Park during the Second World War. He used complicated machines known as bombes, which eliminated enormous numbers of incorrect solutions to the codes so as to arrive at the correct solution. His work is estimated to have shortened the war by two years, but incredibly, his reward was to be prosecuted for homosexuality and obliged to accept injections of synthetic oestrogen which rendered him impotent. He died two years later and it took 57 years before a British government apologised for this barbaric behaviour.

Before the war, in 1936, Turing had already devised a theoretical device called a Turing machine. It consists of an infinitely long tape divided into squares, each bearing a single symbol. Operating according to the directions of an instruction table, a reader moves the tape back and forth, reading one square – and one symbol – at a time. Together with his PhD tutor

Alonzo Church he formulated the Church-Turing thesis, which says that a Turing machine can simulate the logic of any computer algorithm.

(That word "algorithm" crops up a lot in computer science. It simply means a set of rules, or instructions, for a computer to follow. An algorithm is not a programme which tells a computer how to handle a particular situation such as opening a spreadsheet, or calculating the sum of a column of figures. Rather it is a general set of instructions which can be applied to a wide range of data inputs. The algorithm builds an internal model and uses it to make predictions, which it tests against additional data and then refines the model.)

Turing is also famous for inventing a test for artificial consciousness called the Turing Test, in which a machine proves that it is conscious by rendering a panel of human judges unable to determine that it is not (which is essentially the test that we humans apply to each other).

The birth of computing

The first design for a Turing machine was made by Charles Babbage, a Victorian academic and inventor, long before Turing's birth. Babbage never finished the construction of his devices, although working machines have recently been built based on his designs. His Difference Engine (designed in 1822) would carry out basic mathematical functions, and the Analytical Engine (design never completed) would carry out general purpose computation. It would accept as inputs the outputs of previous computations recorded on punch cards. Babbage's collaborator Ada Lovelace has been described as the world's first computer programmer thanks to some of the algorithms she created for the Analytical Engine.

The first electronic digital computer was the Colossus, built by code-breakers at Bletchley Park (although not by Turing). But the first general-purpose computer to be completed was ENIAC (Electronic Numerical Integrator And Computer), built at the Moore School of Electrical Engineering in Philadelphia, and unveiled in 1946. Like so many technological advances, it was funded by the military, and one of its first assignments was a feasibility study of the hydrogen bomb. While working on ENIAC's successor, EDVAC (Electronic Discrete Variable Automatic Computer), the brilliant mathematician and polymath John von Neumann wrote a paper describing an architecture for computers which remains the basis for today's machines.

The Dartmouth Conference

The arrival of computers combined with a series of ideas about thinking by Turing and others led to "the conjecture that every . . . feature of intelligence can in principle be so precisely described that a machine can be made to simulate it." This was the claim of the organisers of a month-long conference at Dartmouth College in New Hampshire in the summer of 1956, which quickly became seen as the foundation event for the science of artificial intelligence. The organisers included John McCarthy, Marvin Minsky, Claude Shannon, and Nathaniel Rochester, all of whom went on to contribute enormously to the field.

In the years following the Dartmouth Conference, some impressive advances were made in AI, and some even more impressive claims were advanced for its potential. Machines were built that could solve high school maths problems, and a programme called Eliza became the world's first chatbot, occasionally fooling users into thinking that it was conscious.

These successes and many others were made possible in part by surprisingly free spending by military research bodies, notably the Defence Advanced Research Projects Agency (DARPA, originally named ARPA), which was established in 1958 by President Eisenhower as part of the shocked reaction in the US to the Soviet achievement of launching Sputnik, the first satellite to be placed into orbit around the Earth.

The optimism of the nascent AI research community in this period is encapsulated by the startling claims made by its leading lights. Herbert Simon said in 1965 that "machines will be capable, within twenty years, of doing any work a man can do,"[5] and Marvin Minksy said two years later that "Within a generation . . . the problem of creating 'artificial intelligence' will substantially be solved."[6] These were hugely over-optimistic claims which with hindsight look like hubris. But hindsight is a wonderful thing, and it is unfair to criticise harshly the pioneers of AI for under-estimating the difficulty of replicating the feats which the human

(5) *The Shape of Automation for Men and Management* by Herbert Simon, 1965

(6) *Computation: Finite and Infinite Machines* by Marvin Minsky, 1967

brain is capable of.

AI winters and springs

When it became apparent that AI was going to take much longer to achieve its goals than originally expected, the funding taps were turned off. There were rumblings of discontent among funding bodies from the late 1960s, and they crystallised in a report written in 1973 by mathematician James Lighthill for the British Science Research Council. A particular problem identified in the Lighthill report is the "combinatorial problem", whereby a simple problem involving two or three variables becomes vast and possibly intractable when the number of variables is increased. Thus simple AI applications which looked impressive in laboratory settings became useless when applied to real-world situations.

From 1974 until around 1980 it was very hard for AI researchers to obtain funding, and this period of relative inactivity which became known as the first AI winter. This bust was followed in the 1980s by another boom, thanks to the advent of expert systems, and the Japanese Fifth Generation Computer Systems project. Expert systems limit themselves to solving narrowly-defined problems from single domains of expertise (for instance, litigation) using vast data banks. They avoid the messy complications of everyday life, and do not tackle the perennial problem of trying to inculcate common sense.

Japan proclaimed its fifth generation project as the successor to the first generation of computing (vacuum tubes), the second (transistors), the third (integrated circuits) and the fourth (microprocessors). It was an attempt to build a powerful presence for the country in the fast-growing computer industry, and also to counteract the perception - widespread at the time - that Japanese firms simply made cheap copies of Western-engineered products. The distinguishing feature of the fifth generation project was its adoption of massively parallel processing – the use of large numbers of processors performing co-ordinated calculations in parallel. Inevitably, Western countries responded by restoring their own funding for major AI projects. Britain launched the £350m Alvey project in 1983 and the following year DARPA set up a Strategic Computer Initiative.

Old hands began to fear that another bubble was forming, and they were proved right in the late 1980s when the funding dried up again. The reason was (again) the under-estimation of the difficulties of the tasks being addressed, and also the fact that desktop computers and what we now call servers overtook mainframes in speed and power, rendering very expensive legacy machines redundant. The boom and bust phenomenon was familiar to economists, with famous examples being Tulipmania in 1637 and the South Sea Bubble in 1720. It has also been a feature of technology introduction since the industrial revolution, seen in canals, railways and telecoms, as well as in the dot-com bubble of the late 1990s.

The second AI winter thawed in the early 1990s, and AI research has been increasingly well funded since then. Some people are worried that the present excitement (and concern) about the progress in AI is merely the latest boom phase, characterised by hype and alarmism, and will shortly be followed by another damaging bust, in which thousands of AI researchers will find themselves out of a job, promising projects will be halted, and important knowledge and insights lost.

However there are reasons for AI researchers to be more sanguine this time round. AI has crossed a threshold and gone mainstream for the simple reason that it works. It is powering services which make a huge difference in people's lives, and which enable companies to make a lot of money: fairly small improvements in AI now make millions of dollars for the companies that introduce them. AI is here to stay because it is lucrative.

1.3 – AI today

AI is everywhere

Artificial intelligence is all around us. People in developed economies interact with AI systems many times every day without being aware of it. If it all suddenly disappeared they would notice, but its omnipresence has become unremarkable, like air.

The most obvious example is your smartphone. It is probably the last inanimate thing you touch before you go to sleep at night and the first thing you touch in the morning. It has more processing power than the computers that NASA used to send Neil Armstrong to the moon in 1969. It uses AI algorithms to offer predictive text and speech recognition services, and these

CALUM CHACE

features improve year by year as the algorithms are improved. Many of the apps we download to our phones also employ AI to make themselves useful to us. The AI in our phones becomes more powerful with each generation of phone as their processing power increases, the bandwidth of the phone networks improve, cloud storage becomes better and cheaper, and we become more relaxed about sharing enough of our personal data for the AIs to "understand" us better.

Many people in the developed economies make several internet searches a day: Google carries out 40,000 searches every second. [7] That is an application of AI.

When you visit a supermarket – or any other kind of store for that matter – the fact that the products you want are on the shelf is significantly due to AI. The supermarkets and their suppliers are continually ingesting huge data feeds and using algorithms to analyse them and predict what we will collectively want to buy, when and where. The retail supply chain is enormously more efficient than it was even a decade ago thanks to these algorithms.

Other consumer-facing companies like Amazon and Netflix wear their AI on their sleeve, tempting us with products and movies based on their algorithms' analysis of what we have chosen in the past. This is the same principle as direct marketing, which has been around for decades, of course. Nowadays the data available and the tools for analysing it are much better, so people living in skyscraper apartments no longer

(7) http://www.internetlivestats.com/google-search-statistics/

14

receive junk email about lawnmowers.

The financial markets make extensive use of AI. High-frequency trading, where computers trade with each other at speeds no human can even follow – never mind participate in – took off in the early 21st century, although it has reportedly fallen back from around two-thirds of all US equity trades at the start of the 2008 credit crunch to around 50% in 2012.[8] There is still confusion about the impact of this on the financial markets. The "flash crash" of 2010, in which the Dow Jones lost almost 10% of its value in a few minutes was initially blamed on high-frequency trading, but later reports claimed that the AIs had actually mitigated the fall. The crash prompted the New York Stock Exchange to introduce "circuit breakers" which suspend trading of a stock whose price moves suspiciously quickly. The financial Armageddon which some pundits forecast has not arrived, and although there will undoubtedly be further shocks to the system, most market participants expect that new AI tools will continue to be developed for and absorbed by what has always been one of the most dynamic and aggressive sectors of the economy.

Hospitals use AI to allocate beds and other resources. Factories use robots – controlled by AI – to automate production and remove people from the most dangerous jobs. Telecoms companies, power generators and other utilities use it to manage the load on their resources.

AI is everywhere you look. Some organisations base their entire existence on it.

(8) http://en.wikipedia.org/wiki/High-frequency_trading

Google is an AI company

Google is an artificial intelligence company. It makes most of its money (and it makes a phenomenal amount of money!) from intelligent algorithms which match adverts with readers and viewers, and it is busily looking for more and more new ways to exploit its world-leading expertise in AI in as many industries as it can manage. The huge collection of servers which comprise the distributed computing platform for the AI which drives the company's numerous services is often called the Google Brain.

Sometimes Google enters a new industry using home-grown talent, as with its famous self-driving cars, and with Calico, which is looking to apply Big Data to healthcare. Other times it acquires companies with the expertise not already found inside Google, or "acqui-hires" their key talent. Its rate of acquisition reached one company a week in 2010, and by the end of 2014 it had acquired 170 of them. Significant industries where Google has engaged by acquiring include smartphones (Android, Motorola), voice over IP telephony (GrandCentral, Phonetic Arts), intelligent house management (Nest Labs, Dropcam and Revolv), robotics (eight robot manufacturers acquired in 2013 alone), publishing (reCAPTCHA and eBook Technologies), banking (TxVia), music (Songza), and drones (Titan Aerospace).

Google's ambitions are startling, and the hurdle for potential acquisition targets is high: they must pass a "toothbrush test", meaning that their services must be potentially useful to most people once or twice every day.

Google also buys companies (and acqui-hires people) which have expertise in AI that is not already applied to a particular industry. Most famously, it paid $500m in January 2014 for DeepMind, a two year-old company employing just 75 people which builds AIs that can learn to play video games better than people. Later in the year it paid another eight-figure sum to hire the seven academics who had established Dark Blue Labs and Vision Factory, two more AI start-ups based in the UK. Before that, in March 2013, it had hired Geoff Hinton, one of the pioneers of machine learning, based in Toronto.

All this activity is partly a matter of economic ambition, but it goes wider than that. Google's founders and leaders want the company to be financially successful, but they also want it to make a difference to people's lives. Founders Larry Page and Sergei Brin think the future will be a better place for humans than the present, and they are impatient for it to arrive.

Philanthropy is a long-established driver for America's business elite – more so than in most other countries. Even the ruthless "robber barons" of the early 20th century who made huge fortunes from railroads, commodities and power used their money to establish major benevolent institutions. Andrew Carnegie pursued wealth aggressively in his early years and spent the last third of his life giving it all away, establishing a pattern followed and advocated by Bill Gates today.

But the Google founders' excitement about the

future is something new. Their famous motto "Don't be evil" is just the start of it. They want to accelerate the progress of technological innovation to transform what it means to be human. Some people are cynical about this, believing that they are simply covering up their corporate greed in philanthropic clothing. I have no privileged information, but I disagree: my sense is that their enthusiasm for the future is genuine. And the pinnacle of it is that they want to build an artificial brain – an AGI. In May 2002 Larry Page said: "Google will fulfil its mission only when its search engine is AI-complete. You guys know what that means? That's artificial intelligence."[9] In December 2012 Google hired the controversial futurist Ray Kurzweil as a director of engineering. Kurzweil, of whom more later, believes that AGI will arrive in 2029, and that the outcome will be very positive.

The other tech giants are in hot pursuit

Facebook, Amazon, Apple, IBM and Microsoft are determined to keep up with Google in the race to develop better and better AI.

Facebook lost out to Google in a competition to buy DeepMind, but in December 2013 it had hired Yann LeCun, a New York-based professor at the forefront of a branch of AI called Deep Learning. It then announced the establishment of a new AI lab which LeCun would run. A year later it hired Vladimir Vapnik, another high-profile AI researcher, from University of London.

For many people, the embodiment of AI today is

(9) *The Big Switch* by Nicholas Carr (p 212)

Siri, Apple's digital personal assistant that first appeared pre-loaded in the iPhone 4S in October 2011. The name is short for Sigrid, a Scandinavian name meaning both "victory" and "beauty". Apple obtained the software in April 2011 by buying Siri, the company which created it, an offshoot of a DARPA-sponsored project. Google responded by launching Google Voice Search (later re-named Google Now) a year later, and Microsoft has launched Cortana.

Microsoft has generally adopted a fast follower strategy rather than being a cutting-edge innovator. In the 21st century it seemed to fall behind the newer tech giants, and was sometimes described as losing relevance. When Satya Nadella became CEO in February 2014 he made strenuous efforts to change this perception, and in July that year Microsoft unveiled Adam, its answer to the Google Brain, running on the company's Azure cloud computing resource. Unusually, Adam uses traditional computer processors (CPUs) rather than the graphics processor units (GPUs) which have become standard where large blocks of data are handled in parallel.

In January 2013, Amazon bought Ivona, a Polish provider of voice recognition and text-to-speech technology. The technology was deployed in various Amazon products including Kindles, and its initially unsuccessful launch into mobile phones. In November 2014 the company announced Echo, a personal assistant which is plugged into mains electricity rather than tethered to a mobile device.

Non-Americans reading this may by now be wondering where the European and Asian players are.

The bald fact is that the technology giants which are major players in AI are almost all US companies. A notable exception is Baidu, founded in 2000 and often referred to as China's Google. It is the leading search engine in China, and in May 2014 it hired Stanford Professor Andrew Ng to head up its new AI lab in Silicon Valley, with a claimed budget of $300m over five years. Ng had been a leading figure in the development of Google Brain and then went on to help found Coursera, Stanford's online education venture.

Big Data

Big Data was the hot topic in business circles in the early 2010s. Businesses and other organisations (especially governments) have massively more data at their disposal than just a few years ago, and it takes considerable effort and ingenuity to figure out what to do with it – if anything.

Without really trying, we are generating and capturing much more data each year than the year before. Thanks to Moore's Law (which we will discuss in chapter 5) the number of cameras, microphones, and sensors of all kinds deployed in the world is growing exponentially. Their quality is improving equally fast. We also leave digital footprints whenever we use social media, smartphones and credit cards.

As well as generating more data, we are quickly expanding our capacity to store and analyse it. Turning Big Data into information and thence into understanding and insight is the job of algorithms – in other words, of AI. Big Data is a manifestation of the expansion of AI.

The gurus of Big Data are Oxford professor Viktor Mayer-Schönberger and *Economist* journalist Kenneth Cukier, who published *Big Data: A Revolution That Will Transform How We Live, Work, and Think* in 2013. Generally optimistic in tone, it offers a series of case studies of ways in which companies and governments are trawling through oceans of data looking for correlations which enable them to understand and influence the behaviour of their customers and citizens. Airlines can work out the best pricing policy for individual seats on each day before a flight. Hollywood studios can avoid making movies which will lose millions of dollars (and perhaps also avoid making original surprise hits).

The book points out some interesting unexpected side-effects of Big Data. It turns out that having more data beats having better data, if what you want is to be able to understand, predict and influence the behaviour of large numbers of people. It also turns out that if you find a reliable correlation then it often doesn't matter if there is a causal link between the two phenomena. We all know of cases where correlation has been mistaken for causation and ineffective or counter-productive policies have been imposed as a result. But if a correlation persists long enough it may provide decision-makers with a useful early warning signal. For instance, a supermarket and an insurance company shared data sets and discovered that men buying red meat and milk during the day were better insurance risks than men buying pasta and petrol late at night. No causal connection could be found: the best hypothesis was that buying pasta and petrol late at night were indicators of negative life changes, such as divorce. The insurance company nevertheless considered offering lower premiums to the meat-buyers.

Mayer-Schönberger and Cukier also addressed the negative aspects of Big Data. Notoriously, government agencies like the NSA and Britain's GCHQ collect and store gargantuan amounts of data on us. They claim this is solely to prevent terrorist atrocities, but can they be trusted? They have been less than forthcoming about what information they are gathering, and why. What happens if the data falls into the hands of even less scrupulous organisations?

In fact it may not be the NSA and GCHQ that we have to worry about. It is reported that they are desperately short of machine learning experts because they are unable to match the salary, lifestyle or moral prestige offered by Google and the other tech giants. This may be less of a handicap for the security agencies in other countries, for example the Third Department of China's People's Liberation Army.[10]

Concerns over privacy can lead to perverse outcomes. Cukier argues that the Ebola epidemic of 2014-15 could have been contained faster – and many lives saved – if phone records had been used to track and analyse the movement of people around West Africa. Fortunately Ebola did not turn into the pandemic that many feared it would, and Cukier urges that we urgently review our priorities regarding

(10) https://en.wikipedia.org/wiki/
People%27s_Liberation_Army#Third_Department

privacy concerns before that does happen. (11)

How good is AI today?

Computers today out-perform humans in many intellectual tasks. They have been better at arithmetic for decades. For many people, a watershed moment was when computers began to beat humans at chess.

IBM's Deep Blue beat the best human chess player in 1997. That match, in which Deep Blue won 3.5 games to Gary Kasparov's 2.5, was not without controversy. Kasparov had beaten the computer four games to two the year before, and he accused IBM of cheating during the second match. He challenged IBM to a re-match, but they refused, and dismantled the machine: it had already achieved the PR coup they were after.

Kasparov went on to hold two general-purpose computers to draws in 2002 and 2003, but by 2005, the best chess computers were unbeatable by humans.

The improvements in computer chess are not due solely – or even mainly – to hardware improvements. Software is advancing rapidly too. Pocket Fritz 4 was released on a smartphone in 2009 and is better than Deep Blue, even though the 20,000 moves it calculates every second is 10,000 times fewer than Deep Blue calculated.

Another major landmark was reached in 2011 when another IBM system, Watson, beat the most successful human players of a TV quiz game, *Jeopardy!*, in which contestants are given the answer and have to deduce the question. IBM said that Watson uses "more than 100

(11) *The Big Switch* by Nicholas Carr (p 212)

different techniques . . . to analyze natural language, identify sources, find and generate hypotheses, find and score evidence, and merge and rank hypotheses." It had access to 200 million pages of information, including the full text of Wikipedia, but it was not online during the contest. The difficulty of the challenge is illustrated by the answer, "A long, tiresome speech delivered by a frothy pie topping" to which the target question (which Watson got right) was "What is a meringue harangue?" After the game, the losing human contestant Ken Jennings famously quipped, "I for one welcome our new robot overlords." [12]

Assembling Watson was an important commercial venture for IBM. It has since invested $1 billion in a new business unit to exploit the technology in health-care and other sectors, and it hopes to generate annual revenues of $10bn within ten years.

Accurate facial recognition was achieved in the mid-2000s, and in 2012 a Google system reviewing randomly-selected pictures on the internet recognised that cats were a category of images. The remarkable thing about this achievement is that the system had never been taught about cats. It was a milestone in machine learning.

In 2011, Nevada became the first US state to allow driverless cars to be tested on its roads. Nevada was joined by Florida and California the following year. By June 2015, Google's small fleet of driverless cars had clocked up a million miles without a single accident that was not caused by a human. Each car is fitted with

(12) https://www.youtube.com/watch?v=Skfw282fJak

a $70,000 LIDAR sensing system and $80,000 of other mapping and analysis equipment. Each has a driver and a Google engineer.

The cars are not perfect. They can only travel on roads where very detailed maps have already been produced. They cannot handle heavy rain or snow, they cannot detect potholes or debris obstructing the road, and they cannot discern between a pedestrian and a policeman indicating for the vehicle to stop.

In November 2012 Microsoft research executive Rick Rashid demonstrated the company's simultaneous translation software at a large presentation. The software rendered his speech in Mandarin in real time, almost flawlessly. The system is now available in 45 languages on a number of Microsoft platforms, including Skype.

One of the most impressive recent demonstrations of AI functionality was DeepMind's presentation at Lake Tahoe in December 2013 of an AI system teaching itself to play old-style Atari video games like Breakout and Pong. These are games which previous AI systems have found hard to play because they involve hand-to-eye co-ordination. The most striking thing about DeepMind's system is that it solves problems and masters skills without being specifically programmed to do so. It shows true general learning ability.

The system was not given instructions for how to play the game well, or even told the rules and purpose of the game: it was simply rewarded when it played well and not rewarded when it played less well. The system's first attempt at each game was disastrous but by playing continuously for 24 hours or so it worked out – through trial and error – the subtleties in the gameplay and scoring system, and played the game better than the best human player. It took longer to master Space Invaders, where the winning strategies are less obvious.

DeepMind's founder, Demis Hassabis, remarked that it is easier to experiment with AI using video games than robots because it avoids the messy business of hydraulics, power and gravity that dealing with the real world entails. But the hand-eye co-ordination could well prove useful with real-world robots as well as video games. Perhaps part of the attraction of DeepMind to Google was the potential to accelerate the development of all those robot companies it had bought.

The science of what we can't yet do

A famous cartoon shows a man in a small room writing notes to stick on the wall behind him. Each note shows an intellectual task which computers are unable to carry out. On the floor there is a growing pile of discarded notes – notes which show tasks which computers now carry out better than humans. The notes of the floor include "arithmetical calculations", "play chess", "recognise faces", "compose music in the style of Bach", "play table tennis". The notes on the wall include tasks which no computer can do today, including "demonstrate common sense", but also some tasks which they now can, such as "drive cars", "translate speech in real time".

The man in the cartoon has a nervous expression:

he is perturbed by the rising tide of tasks which computers can perform better than humans. Of course it may be that there will come a time the notes stop moving from the wall to the floor. Perhaps computers will never demonstrate common sense. Perhaps they will never report themselves to be conscious. Perhaps they will never decide to revise their goals. But given their startling progress to date and the weakness of the *a priori* arguments that conscious machines cannot be created (which we will review in chapter 4), it seems unwise to bet too heavily on it.

A lot of people were surprised when Stephen Hawking and Elon Musk said in 2014 that the future of artificial intelligence was something to be concerned about. Both men applauded the achievements of AI research, and the benefits it has delivered. They went on to ask what will happen if and when computers become smarter than people, and we find that we have created a super-intelligence.

We will look at the detail of what they said later on, but putting that to one side for the moment along with the question of whether they are right to be concerned, why were so many people surprised? The rapid progress of AI has not been hidden, and the possibility of a negative outcome has been described in novels and movies for many years.

One reason why people were surprised to hear the warnings that AI could be very dangerous in the medium-term future is that functionality provided by artificial intelligence tends to get re-named as something else as soon as it has been realised.

27

Although iPhones and Android phones are called "smartphones", we don't tend to think of them as instantiations of artificial intelligence. We don't tend to think of the logistical systems of the big supermarkets as examples of AI. In effect, artificial intelligence is re-defined every time a breakthrough is achieved. Computer scientist Larry Tesler pointed out that this means AI is being defined as "whatever hasn't been done yet", an observation which has become known as Tesler's Theorem, or the AI effect.

For many years, people believed that computers would never beat humans at chess. When it finally happened, it was dismissed as mere computation – mere brute force, and not proper thinking at all. The rebarbative American linguistics professor Noam Chomsky declared that a computer programme beating a human at chess as no more interesting than a bulldozer winning an Olympic gold at weight-lifting.

He has a point. Computers cannot do what most people probably regard as the core of their own cognition. They are not (as far as we know) self-conscious. They cannot reflect rationally on their goals and adjust them. They do not (as far as we know) get excited about the prospect of achieving their goals. They do not (we believe) actually understand what they are doing when they play a game of chess, for instance.

In this sense it is fair to say that what AI systems do is "mere computation". Then again, a lot of what the human brain does is "mere computation", and it has enabled humans to achieve some wondrous things. It is not unreasonable that humans want to preserve some space for themselves at the top of the intellectual tree. But to dismiss everything that AI has achieved as not intelligent, and to conclude – as some people do – that AI research has made no progress since its early days in the 1950s and 1960s is frankly ridiculous.

CHAPTER 2
TOMORROW'S AI

2.1 – A day in the life

Julia woke up feeling rested and refreshed. This was unremarkable: she had done so ever since Hermione, her digital assistant, had been upgraded to monitor her sleep patterns and wake her at the best stage in her sleep cycle. But Julia could still remember what it was like to wake up to the sound of an alarm crashing through REM sleep and she felt grateful as she stretched her arms and smelled the coffee which Hermione had prepared.

Traffic feeds indicated that the roads were quiet, so with a few minutes in hand, Hermione updated her on her key health indicators – blood pressure, cholesterol levels, percentage body fat, insulin levels and the rest. Julia had long since stopped feeling disturbed by the idea of the tiny monitors that nestled in all parts of her body, including her bloodstream, her eye fluids, her internal organs, and her mouth.

She slipped into the outfit that she and Hermione

had put together last night with the aid of some virtual wardrobe browsing and a bit of online shopping. An airborne drone had dropped off the new dress while Julia was asleep; selecting the right size was rarely a problem now that virtual mannequins were supported by most retailers. The finishing touch was an intriguing necklace which Julia had her 3D printer produce overnight in a colour which complemented the dress perfectly, based on a design sent down by her sister in Edinburgh.

During the drive to the station, Julia read a couple of the items which Hermione had flagged for her in the morning's newsfeed, along with some gossip about a friend who had recently relocated to California. With a gesture inside the holosphere projected by Hermione for the purpose, Julia OK'd the micropayments to the newsfeeds. Half an hour later, she smiled to herself as her self-driving car slotted itself perfectly into one of the tight spaces in the station car park. It was a while since she had attempted the manoeuvre herself; she knew she would not have executed it so smoothly even when she used to do her own driving. She certainly wouldn't be able to do it now that she was so out of practice.

The train arrived soon after she reached the platform (perfect timing by her car, again) and Hermione used the display in Julia's augmented reality (AR) contact lenses to highlight the carriage with the most empty seats, drawing on information from sensors inside the train. As Julia boarded the carriage the display highlighted the best seat to choose, based on her travelling preferences and the convenience of disembarkation at the other end of the journey.

Julia noticed that most of her fellow passengers wore opaque goggles: they were watching entertainments with fully immersive virtual reality (VR) sets. She didn't join them. She was going to be spending at least a couple of hours in full virtual reality during the meeting today and she had a personal rule to limit the numbers of hours spent in VR each day.

Instead she kept her AR lenses in and gazed out of the window. The train took her through parts of the English countryside where she could choose between overlays from several different historical periods. Today she chose the Victorian era, and enjoyed watching how the railway she was travelling was under construction in some parts, with gangs of labourers laying down tracks. She marvelled at that kind of work being done by humans rather than machines.

Hermione interrupted her reverie, reminding Julia that tomorrow was her mother's birthday. Hermione displayed a list of suggested presents for Julia to order for delivery later today, along with a list of the presents she had sent in recent years to make sure there was no tactless duplication. Julia chose the second gift on the list and authorised payment along with Hermione's suggested greeting.

That done, Hermione left her to indulge in her historical browsing for the rest of the journey. The augmented views became increasingly interesting as the train reached the city outskirts, and huge Victorian construction projects unfolded across south

London. Julia noticed that the content makers had improved the views since the last time she watched it, adding a host of new characters, and a great deal more information about the buildings in the accompanying virtual menus.

When she reached her office she had a half hour to spare before the meeting started, so she crafted an introductory message to an important potential new client. She used the latest psychological evaluation algorithm to analyse all the target's publicly available statements, including blog posts, emails, comments and tweets. After reading the resulting profile she uploaded it into Hermione to help with the drafting. Hermione suggested various phrases and constructions which helped Julia to keep the message formal, avoiding metaphors and any kind of emotive language. The profile suggested that the target liked all claims to be supported by evidence, and didn't mind receiving long messages as long as they were relevant and to the point.

It was time for the conference call – the main reason she had come into the office today. She was meeting several of her colleagues in VR because they were based in ten different locations around the world, and the topic was important and sensitive, so they wanted the communication to be as rich as possible, with all of them being able to see each other's facial expressions and body language in detail. Her VR rig at home wasn't sophisticated enough to participate in this sort of call.

A competitor had just launched a completely automated version of one of Julia's company's major service lines in two countries, and it would probably be rolled out worldwide within a couple of weeks. Julia and her colleagues had to decide whether to abandon the service line, or make the necessary investment to follow suit in automating it – which meant retraining a hundred members of staff, or letting them go.

As always, Julia was grateful to Hermione for discreetly reminding her of the personal details of the colleagues in the meeting that she knew least well. In the small talk at the start and the end of the call she was able to enquire about their partners and children by name. It didn't bother her at all that their ability to do the same was probably thanks at least in part to their own digital assistants.

Several of the participants in the call did not speak English as their first language, so their words were translated by a real-time machine translation system. The words Julia heard them speak did not exactly match the movement of their mouths, but the system achieved a very believable representation of their vocal characteristics and their inflections.

A couple of times during the call Hermione advised Julia to slow down, or get to the point faster, using the same psychological evaluation software which had helped to craft the sales message earlier, and also using body language and facial expression evaluation software.

After the meeting Julia had lunch with a friend who worked in a nearby office. Hermione advised her against the crème brulee because it would take her beyond her target sugar intake for the day. Julia took a little guilty pleasure in ignoring the advice, and she was sure the dessert tasted better as a result. Hermione made no comment, but adjusted Julia's target for mild aerobic exercise for the day, and set a reminder to recommend a slightly longer time brushing and flossing before bed.

Before heading back to the office, Julia and her friend went shopping for shoes. She was about to buy a pair of killer heels when Hermione advised her that the manufacturer was on an ethical blacklist that Julia subscribed to.

Back in the office, Julia set about re-configuring the settings on one of the company's lead generation websites. The site used evolutionary algorithms which continuously tested the impact of tiny changes in language, colour and layout, adjusting the site every few seconds to optimise its performance according to the results. This was a never-ending process because the web itself was changing all the time, and a site which was perfectly optimised at one moment would be outmoded within minutes unless it was re-updated. The internet was a relentlessly Darwinian environment, where the survival of the fittest demanded constant vigilance.

Re-configuring the site's settings was a delicate affair because any small error would be compounded rapidly by the evolutionary algorithm, which could quickly lead to unfortunate consequences. She decided to do it with a sophisticated new type of software she had read about the day before. The software provider had supplied detailed instructions to follow with AR glasses. She went through the signup, login and operating sequences carefully, comparing the results with the images shown in her glasses.

By the time Julia was on the train home it was getting dark. She asked Hermione to review the recording of her day and download the new app her friend had recommended in passing at lunchtime. Then she queued up two short videos and four new songs for the drive from the station to her house. She was the only person to get off the train at her home station, so she asked Hermione to display the camera feeds on the two routes she could take from the platform to her car. There was no-one on the bridge over the tracks but there was someone loitering in a shadowy part of the underpass. She took the bridge, even though it was a slightly longer route.

When she reached her car she checked that the delivery drone had opened her car's boot successfully and dropped the groceries there before re-locking it with the remote locking code. Happy in the full possession of her vegetables, she drove home, humming along to Joni Mitchell.

2.2 – Converting information into knowledge – at different speeds

The science fiction writer William Gibson is reported as saying that "The future is already here – it's just not evenly distributed."[13] Most of the things mentioned in the short story above are already available in prototype and early incarnations, and the rest is firmly

(13) *The Economist*, December 4, 2003

under development – some of it as part of the so-called "internet of things". It could take anywhere from five to fifteen years for you to have working versions of all of them.

Some people will think the life described above is frightening, perhaps de-humanised. It is likely that more people will welcome the assistance, and of course generations to come will simply take it for granted. As Douglas Adams said, anything invented after you're thirty-five is against the natural order of things, anything invented between when you're fifteen and thirty-five is new and exciting, and anything that is in the world when you're born is just a natural part of the way the world works. [14]

Of course there is no guarantee that the future will work out this way – in fact the details are bound to be different. For example we don't yet know whether the myriad devices connecting up to the Internet of Things will communicate with us directly, or via personal digital assistants like Hermione. Will you be reminded to take your pill in the morning because its bottle starts glowing, or will Hermione alert you? No doubt the outcome will seem obvious in hindsight.

It has been said that all industries are now part of the information industry – or heading that way. Much of the cost of developing a modern car – and much of the quality of its performance – lies in the software that controls it.

Demis Hassabis has said that AI converts information into knowledge, which he sees as empowering

(14) Douglas Adams, *The Salmon of Doubt*

people. The mission statement of Google, the new owner of his company, is to organise the world's information and make it universally accessible and useful. For many of us, most of the tasks that we perform each day can be broken down into four fundamental skills: looking, reading, writing, and integrating knowledge. AI is already helping with all these tasks in a wide range of situations, and its usefulness is spreading and deepening.

Marketers used to observe that much of the value of a product lay in the branding – the emotional associations which surrounded it. The same is now true of the information which surrounds it. You might think that the commercial success of a product as physical as say, skincream does not rely on the provision of information to its consumers. Increasingly that is wrong. Consumers have access to staggering amounts of information about skincare, and many of them want to know how each product they might use would affect their overall regime. In a world of savvy consumers, the manufacturer which provides the most concise, easy-to-navigate advice is going to win market share.

From supermarket supply chains to consumer goods to construction to exploring for minerals and oil, the ability to crunch bigger and bigger data sets and make sense of them is improving pretty much every type of human endeavour. Kevin Kelly, the founder of Wired magazine, said the business plans of the next 10,000 startups are easy to predict: "Take X and add AI."[15] To coin a phrase, blessed are the geeks, for they shall

(15) http://www.wired.com/2014/10/future-of-artificial-intelligence/

inherit the Earth.

Healthcare is an interesting industry in this respect, because it has so far appeared to lag behind the general trend to improved performance from better information. It has been observed that our healthcare systems are really sick-care systems, often spending 90% of the amount they ever spend on an individual during the final year of their lives. We all know that prevention is better than cure, and that problems are most easily solved when identified early on, but we don't run our healthcare systems that way.

Two major revolutions are about to sweep across the healthcare horizon, and we will all benefit. One is the availability of small instruments which attach to our smartphones, enabling each of us to diagnose early symptoms of disease, and transmit relevant data to remote clinicians. These instruments are the result of cheaper and better sensors, and the application of AI algorithms and human ingenuity to huge data sets. They will cut out millions of time-consuming and expensive visits to doctors, and enable us to tilt sick-care towards healthcare.

The other revolution is the ability to anticipate and forestall medical problems by analysing our genomes. The Human Genome Project was completed back in 2003, but it soon turned out that although sequencing our DNA was an essential first step to enabling the practical improvements to healthcare we hoped for, it was not enough. We needed to understand epigenetics too: the changes in our cells that are caused by factors above and beyond our DNA sequence. The application of AI algorithms to the data which scientists are generating about gene expression are now bringing those improvements within reach.

There is almost no aspect of life today which is not being improved by artificial intelligence. It is important to bear that in mind as we look at the potential downsides of this enormously powerful technology, and avoid a backlash which could prevent us benefiting from those improvements.

CHAPTER 3
FROM DIGITAL DISRUPTION TO ECONOMIC SINGULARITY

AI is a powerful tool, and it is growing more powerful at an exponential rate. In the last two chapters we saw how it is improving our lives enormously, supporting us in carrying out a wide range of professional and personal tasks, providing information and analysis to make us more efficient and more effective. But this improvement means change, and change is usually uncomfortable. There are concerns that it is automating our jobs out of existence, and that this will increase rapidly in the coming few years. There are concerns that AI is de-humanising war, and there are calls for a ban on the development of machines which make life-or-death decisions on the battlefield. And there are concerns that the digital disruption of various industries is placing millions of people around the world at a sudden and unexpected disadvantage.

3.1 – Digital disruption

Business buzzwords

In the early 2010s the hottest buzzword (buzz-phrase?) in business circles was Big Data. As always, there was a good reason for this, even if the endless repetition of the phrase became tiresome. Executives woke up to the fact that the huge amount of information they had about their customers and their targets could finally be analysed and turned into useful insights thanks to the reduced cost of very powerful (parallel processing) computers and clever AI algorithms. At long last, consumer goods manufacturers could do better than simply grouping their customers into zipcodes, or broad socio-demographic tribes. They could find tiny sub-clusters of people with identical requirements for product variants and delivery routes, and communicate with them in a timely and accurate fashion.

Previous disruption by technological innovation

In the mid-2010s the buzzword is digital disruption, and again there is good reason for it. Disruption of businesses and whole industries by technological innovation is nothing new. If you visit Chile's Atacama desert you can see substantial ghost towns which were abandoned pretty much overnight in October 1908. For decades before then, thousands of men laboured in the hot sun, digging saltpetre (nitrate) out of the ground. Apart from guano from Peru, Chile's saltpetre was the world's only source of nitrogen in solid form.

Nitrogen is a basic nutrient for plants, and it makes up 78% of the atmosphere, but its gaseous form is hard for farmers to use.

On 13th October 1908, a German chemist named Fritz Haber filed a patent for ammonia, having managed to solidify nitrogen in a useful and stable form for the first time: three atoms of hydrogen and one of nitrogen. Salptre became uneconomic overnight, and you can see trains that were carrying loads of it to the port which were simply abandoned mid-journey.

Today's disruption is caused by the digital revolution – the internet, in short – and it is unusual in that it is affecting so many industries simultaneously. During the dotcom boom and bust at the turn of the century there was much talk of companies being "disintermediated" by the internet, and a continuing example of that is the publishing industry, where publishers no longer dictate whose books get read because Amazon has enabled authors to publish themselves.

Kodak

The poster child of digital disruption is Kodak. At its peak in the late 1980s it employed 145,000 people and had annual sales of $19bn. Its 1,300-acre campus in Rochester, New York had 200 buildings, and George Eastman was as revered there a few decades ago as Steve Jobs is in Silicon Valley today.

Kodak's researchers invented digital photography, but its executives could not see a way to make the technology commercially viable without cannibalising their immensely lucrative consumer film business. So other companies stepped in to market digital cameras: film sales started to fall 20-30% a year in the early 2000s, even before the arrival of smartphones. Kodak is often accused of being complacent but the dilemma it faced was almost impossible. In the classic phrase of the dotcom era, it needed to eat its own babies, and this it could not do.

Instead it spent a fortune entering the pharmaceuticals industry, paying $5.1 billion for Sterling Drug, and another fortune entering the home printing industry. Both ventures were unsuccessful, and Kodak filed for bankruptcy in 2012, emerging from it a year later as a mere shadow of its former glory. Today it has annual sales of $2bn and employs 8,000 people. 80 of the 200 campus buildings have been demolished and 59 others have been sold off. Its market capitalisation is about $800 million, one-sixth that of GoPro, a maker of (digital) cameras for extreme sports that was founded in 2002.

Peer-to-peer

A new business model which is generating a lot of column inches for the idea of digital disruption is peer-to-peer commerce, the leading practitioners of which are AirBnB and Uber. Both were founded in San Francisco, of course – in 2008 and 2009 respectively.

The level of investor enthusiasm for the peer-to-peer model is demonstrated by comparing AirBnB's market cap of $20bn in March 2015 with Hyatt's market cap of $8.4bn. Hyatt has over 500 hotels around the world and revenues of $4bn. AirBnB, with 13 members of staff, owns no hotels and its revenues in March 2015 were around \$250m. Uber's rise has been even more dramatic: its market cap reached \$50bn in May 2015.

This sort of growth is unsettling for competitors. Taxi drivers around the world protest that Uber is putting them out of business by competing unfairly, since (they claim) its drivers can flout safety regulations with impunity. Hoteliers have tried to have AirBnB banned from the cities where they operate, sometimes successfully.

A sub-industry of authors and consultants has sprung up, offering to help businesses cope with this disruption. One of its leading figures is Peter Diamandis, who is also a co-founder of Silicon Valley's Singularity University. Diamandis talks about the Six Ds of digital disruption, arguing that the insurgent companies are:

1. **Digitized**, exploiting the ability to share information at the speed of light

2. **Deceptive**, because their growth, being exponential, is hidden for some time and then seems to accelerate almost out of control (we will look at exponential growth in chapter 5)

3. **Disruptive**, because they steal huge chunks of market share from incumbents

4. **Dematerialized**, in that much of their value lies in the information they provide rather than anything physical, which means their distribution costs can be minimal or zero

5. **Demonetized**, in that they can provide for

nothing things which customers previously had
to pay for dearly

6. **Democratized**, in that they make products and
services which were previously the preserve of
the rich (like cellphones) available to the many.

It is odd that Diamandis didn't add a seventh D, for
Data-driven. The disruptive companies exploit the
massive amounts of data that are now available, and
the computational capacity to analyse them.

The task for business leaders is to work out whether
their industry can be disrupted by this sort of insurgent (hint: almost certainly yes) and whether they can
do the disruption themselves rather than being left
standing in rubble like Kodak.

Digital disruption is devastating partly because
it enables competitors to undercut your product and
service price dramatically. That cheapness also means
there will be many more potential disrupters because
the barriers to entry are disappearing. Small wonder
that Monitor, the business consultancy established by
Michael Porter to advise companies how to erect those
barriers, went bankrupt.

Business leaders often know what they need to do:
set up small internal teams of their most talented people to brainstorm potential disruptions and then go
ahead and do the disrupting first. These teams need
high-level support and freedom from the usual metrics
of return on investment, at least for a while. The theory
is fairly easy but putting it into practice is hard: most
will need external help, and many will fail.

Of course the disrupters can also be disrupted. A service called La'Zooz[16] is planned, based on the blockchain technology you will have heard about in connection with Bitcoin, which may provide serious competition for Uber.

3.2 – Killer robots

It is not only commerce where AI is threatening disruption. Human Rights Watch and other organisations are concerned that within a decade or two, fully autonomous weapons will be available to military forces with deep pockets.[17] They argue that lethal force should never be delegated to machines because they can never be morally responsible. This moral argument may be simply untrue if and when we create machines whose cognitive abilities match or exceed those of humans in every respect, i.e. artificial general intelligences, which are the subject of the rest of this book.

But long before then we will face other dilemmas. If wars can be fought by robots, would that not be better than human slaughter? And when robots can discriminate between combatants and civilian bystanders better than human soldiers, who should pull the trigger?

It has been argued that slaughter-free war will make starting a war an easier decision for beleaguered populist politicians. There is another possibility, though. Military leaders in an age where most combatants are robots will have a clearer idea of whether their forces

(16) http://lazooz.org/
(17) https://www.hrw.org/reports/2012/11/19/losing-humanity

are a match for those of the opposition. The leaders with the weaker forces may feel less inclined to start a war they can be fairly confident they will lose.

3.3 – Economic singularity

In the medium term, AI presents economists, business people and policy makers with an even bigger concern than digital disruption. It may render most of us unemployed, and indeed unemployable, because our jobs have been automated.

Automation

Automation has been a feature of human civilisation since at least the early industrial revolution. In the 15th century, Dutch workers threw their shoes into textile looms to break them. (Their shoes were called sabots, which is a possible etymology for the word "saboteur".) The development of engines powered by steam and then coal raised automation to a new level. The classic example is the mechanisation of agriculture, which accounted for 41% of US employment in 1900, and only 2% in 2000.

In the late 20th century, automation came mainly in the form of robots, particularly in the automotive and electrical / electronic industries – and this is set to accelerate. Robots are peripherals – physical extensions of AI systems. Despite the recession, sales of robots grew at 10% a year from 2008 to 2013, when 178,000 industrial robots were sold worldwide. China became the biggest market, installing 37,000 robots compared with 30,000 in the USA. [18]

So the process of automation has been familiar in manual labour jobs for many years. It has also rendered obsolete large numbers of clerical jobs. As we saw in chapter 1, the word "computer" originally meant a person who does calculations, but the days when offices were filled with battalions of young (usually male) human computers are long gone. The humble PC has also removed the need for legions of (usually female) secretaries.

The fear that automation would lead to mass unemployment is not new. In 1930, the British economist John Maynard Keynes wrote "We are being afflicted with a new disease of which some readers may not yet have heard the name, but of which they will hear a great deal in the years to come – namely technological unemployment. This means unemployment due to our discovery of means of economising the use of labour outrunning the pace at which we can find new uses for labour." [19] Decades later, in the late 1970s, a powerful BBC Horizon documentary called *Now the Chips are Down* alerted a new generation to the idea (and showcased some truly appalling ties.) [20]

Up to now the replacement of humans by machines has been a gradual process. Although it has been painful for each individual who was dismissed

(18) http://www.ifr.org/industrial-robots/statistics/

(19) "Economic possibilities for our grandchildren": http://www.econ.yale.edu/smith/econ116a/keynes1.pdf

(20) https://www.youtube.com/watch?v=HW5Fvk8FNOQ

from a particular job, there was generally the chance to retrain, or find new work elsewhere. The idea that each job lost to automation equates to a person rendered permanently unemployed is known as the Luddite Fallacy.

This is unfair to the Luddites, who weren't advancing a sociological thesis about the long-term effects of technology. They were simply protesting about the very real danger of starvation in the short term. It is also not true that Maynard Keynes argued that automation would destroy jobs any time soon. The essay quoted above goes on to say, "But this is only a temporary phase of maladjustment. All this means in the long run that mankind is solving its economic problem. I would predict that the standard of life in progressive countries one hundred years hence will be between four and eight times as high as it is to-day . . . [and] it would not be foolish to contemplate the possibility of far greater progress still." Keynes was a great optimist, and he thought the problem was not unemployment *per se*, but how people would find meaning in lives of pure leisure. "To those who sweat for their daily bread, leisure is a longed-for sweet – until they get it."

This time it's different?

Some people argue that soon, people automated out of a job may not find new employment, thanks to the rapid advances in machine learning, and the availability of increasingly powerful and increasingly portable computers.

MIT professors Andrew McAfee and Erik

Brynjolfsson have published two seminal books on the subject: *Race Against the Machine*, and *The Second Machine Age*. A report in September 2013 by the Oxford Martin School estimated that 45% of American jobs would disappear in the next 20 years, in two waves. [21] The first would attack relatively low-skilled jobs in transportation and administration. Some of this would come from self-driving vehicles, which are likely to appear on our roads in significant numbers from 2017. Some 30 US cities will be experimenting with self-driving cars by the end of 2016, for instance. [22]

There are 3.5 million truck drivers in the US alone, [23] 650,000 bus drivers [24] and 230,000 taxi drivers. [25] There are numerous hurdles to be overcome before all these jobs become vulnerable. At the time of writing, Google's self-driving cars have travelled a million miles without causing an accident. As we saw in chapter 1 they are not perfect, but none of the challenges facing them look insurmountable: Google was recently awarded a patent for a system which can tell whether a cyclist is signalling a turn. Politicians worldwide have understood that they need to agree and implement

(21) http://www.oxfordmartin.ox.ac.uk/downloads/academic/The_Future_of_Employment.pdf

(22) http://www.dailymail.co.uk/sciencetech/article-2981946/Self-driving-cars-30-cities-2017-Pilot-projects-aims-mass-roll-driverless-vehicles-safe-they.html

(23) http://www.alltrucking.com/faq/truck-drivers-in-the-usa/

(24) http://www.bls.gov/ooh/transportation-and-material-moving/bus-drivers.htm

(25) http://www.bls.gov/ooh/transportation-and-material-moving/taxi-drivers-and-chauffeurs.htm

policies and procedures to cope with the arrival of this technology.

(The impetus to introduce self-driving cars is enormous. Around 1.2m lives are lost on the world's roads each year and most of these deaths are due to driver error. Self-driving cars don't get tired, distracted or drunk. Accidents are also a major cause of traffic congestion, so average journey times would be significantly reduced if most cars were self-driving. Car-sharing is expected to become more common, and parking should become much easier. There are always unforeseen consequences, of course. In 2014, Los Angeles generated $160m from parking violations, much of which could have to come from somewhere else in future.)

The second wave of automation forecast by the Oxford Martin School report will affect jobs in the heartland of the middle and upper-middle class: professional occupations like medicine and the law, managerial jobs, and even in the arts. The claim is that systems like IBM's Watson will progress from being decision-support systems to being decision-taking systems. As the ability of machines to turn raw data into information and then insight improves, the space remaining for a human to add value shrinks and eventually disappears.

In this vision, a requirement for creativity is not necessarily a defence against automation. Computers can already write sports articles for newspapers which readers cannot distinguish from pieces penned by humans. A computer system called Iamus in Malaga, Spain, produces chamber music which experts cannot identify as automated. [26]

What will the impact on society be if nearly half of all today's jobs disappear in a mere two decades? Some people argue that the fears are over-done because technology is not actually advancing as fast as the excitable folk in Silicon Valley suppose. It is true that economists have long struggled to record the productivity improvements that would be expected from the massive investments in information technology of the last half-century; this failure prompted economist Robert Solow to remark back in 1987 that "You can see the computer age everywhere but in the productivity statistics."

(Of the various explanations for this phenomenon, the one which seems most plausible to me is that there is an increase in productivity, but for some reason our economic measurements don't catch it. When I started work in the early 1980s we used to spend hours each day looking for information by searching in files and phoning each other up. Now we have Google and the almost infinite filing cabinet known as the internet.)

Sceptics also observe that automation is rarely as straightforward as it appears. For instance, they claim that self-driving lorries and buses will still need attendants to cater for the unexpected circumstances that life throws up, as well as to load and unload people and goods. They could point to the example of aircraft, which have been flying by wire for decades, but which still have human pilots on board, even though the AI

(26) http://www.cristo-barrios.com/discografia/iamus-2/?lang=en

in typical passenger planes is now so sophisticated that the pilot only has hands-on control for three minutes each flight.[27] But a plane costs millions of dollars, carries hundreds of people, and is effectively a flying bomb. We might well insist on human oversight in planes (including a second human to oversee the first human) while not requiring it in taxis.

When it comes to automating the lawyer and the doctor, the sceptic might think that AI will relieve them of the more mundane work, leaving just the most creative, the most intellectually stimulating tasks for humans to address. An optimistic sceptic might argue that we will no longer have to queue to see a doctor, or pay so much to see a top lawyer, because automation will de-clutter their calendars. Perhaps we can get round the problem of how professionals acquire their skills when the AI is doing all the grunt work which currently provides the training for junior doctors and lawyers. But harder to escape is the thought that the piece of analysis or decision-making that the AI can't do today, it may well be able to do tomorrow, or the next day.

Rapid job churn or economic singularity

If computers steal our old jobs, perhaps we can invent lots of new ones? In the past, people whose jobs were automated turned their hands to more value-adding activity, and the net result was higher overall productivity. The children of people who did back-breaking

(27) http://www.theatlantic.com/magazine/archive/2013/11/
the-great-forgetting/309516/

farm work for subsistence wages moved into the cities where they earned a little more doing mundane jobs in offices and factories. Their great-grandchildren now work as social media marketers and user experience designers – jobs which their great-grandparents could not have imagined. Perhaps our children will also be doing jobs that we could not anticipate today. (Emotion coaches? Dream wranglers?)

Probably not. Martin Ford, who has written extensively on technological unemployment, argues that in 2014, 90% of the USA's 150m workers were doing jobs which already existed 100 years earlier. [28]

Even if we can keep inventing new types of employment, will the rate of churn be too fast for us to keep up? Will we all be able to change our career annually or every six months as computers keep stealing our old ones? The rapid growth of online education (the MOOC, or Massive Open Online Courses revolution) means that employees can re-skill themselves faster than ever before, and for free. But we may lose this race up the value chain if AI systems are clambering up it as fast as we are, or faster.

So there may well come a time when a majority of jobs can be performed more effectively, efficiently or economically by an AI than they can be done by a human. This could be called the economic singularity, [29] by analogy with the technological singularity

(28) https://twitter.com/MFordFuture/status/606939607356219392/photo/1

(29) http://www.reddit.com/r/Futurology/comments/34u1a9/tech-nostism_the_ideology_of_futurology/People also talk about a financial singularity arriving if and when cryptocurrencies like Bitcoin based on the

which we will discuss in chapter 6. During the Great Depression, unemployment peaked at 25% of the US population in 1933, and the resulting trauma is seared into the political memory even now. Social provision for the unemployed has improved greatly since then, and countries (for instance in southern Europe) with similar levels of unemployment today don't seem so desperate. But if the day dawns when everyone acknowledges that more than half the population will never work again, the result will surely be a political and social crisis sufficient to oblige governments everywhere to do something about it.

UBI and VR

If and when the economic singularity arrives, we may need to institute what is now called the Universal Basic Income (UBI). This is a payment available to all citizens as of right, providing everyone with the living standard of today's middle-class American. The optimistic scenario is that AI-powered robots do all the work, creating an economy of what Peter Diamandis calls radical abundance, leaving humans to pursue self-fulfilment by reading, writing, talking, playing sports and undertaking adventures. Or perhaps playing endless video games in immersive virtual realities. Martin Ford envisages this as a modification to the market economy, with the UBI being funded by taxes on the rich. An alternative is some form of socialism, whereby the means of production – the AI systems and their peripherals, the

blockchain technology disrupt traditional banking. Are we perhaps nearing peak singularity, or a singularity singularity?

robots – will be taken into common ownership.

UBI is a noble vision, but it leaves three large problems outstanding: the allocation of scarce resources, the creation of meaning, and the transition.

Even if radical abundance is possible without consuming and polluting the entire planet, there will still be scarce resources. Who gets the beachfront property with the palm trees and the white sand? Who gets the original Monet? When the economic singularity arrives do we simply declare that the financial game of musical chairs is over, and everyone's asset position is frozen – the rich stay rich forever, and the poor stay poor? Or would we introduce some kind of time-sharing arrangement? Or perhaps there will be a tiny elite working in those few remaining jobs that computers can't yet do, and they will enjoy the best goods and services?

These thoughts are leading some people to worry that a dystopia is inevitable, in which an elite preys on the majority, using powerfully intrusive technologies to impose a truly nightmarish 1984 scenario.

Perhaps Virtual Reality will ride to the rescue. Indeed, perhaps VR is a necessary element of radical abundance. In real life, not everyone can have the beachfront property and a beautiful spouse. In VR, given a generous supply of bandwidth, everyone can.

What about meaning? A lot of people would be more than happy with a life of ease, playing golf and video games, organising social events. Or at least they think they would. We've all heard the story of the exhausted executive who yearns for his retirement but goes right back to work after about six months because his life feels meaningless without it. It is true that there are many ways to give a life meaning, but for many people it is work of one kind or another, perhaps paid and perhaps not. But again, what happens if there is nothing that we humans can do that an AI cannot do better? A lot of us are going to find that difficult.

Let's say that radical abundance is possible, and the need for meaning can be satisfied. The third big problem is getting from here to there. It will involve enormous disruption to existing economic and social systems, and also to cherished ideologies. Can we effect this transition peacefully, or will there be social breakdown and sporadic violence, sufficient perhaps to snatch the prize from our grasp, throwing us back into dystopia?

Which of these scenarios will come true – or will there be another, currently unsuspected outcome? The answer, as so often in matters concerning AI, is that no-one yet knows, but the most likely outcome is one that no-one has precisely predicted. History doesn't repeat itself, and even though it sometimes rhymes, the rhyme is often irregular and impossible to forecast, although it seems natural in hindsight. As we saw in the introduction to this book, nobody suggested thirty years ago that we would have powerful AIs in our pockets in the form of telephones, even though now that it has happened it seems a natural and logical development.

PART TWO: AGI

Artificial General Intelligence

CHAPTER 4
CAN WE BUILD AN AGI?

4.1 – Is it possible in principle?

The three biggest questions about artificial general intelligence (AGI) are:

1. Can we build one?

2. If so, when?

3. Will it be safe?

The first of these questions is the closest to having an answer, and that answer is "probably, as long as we don't go extinct first". The reason for this is that we already have proof that it is possible for a general intelligence to be developed using very common materials. This so-called "existence proof" is our own brains. They were developed by a powerful but inefficient process called evolution.

Evolution: the slow, inefficient way to develop a brain

Evolution does not have a purpose or a goal. It is merely a by-product of the struggle for survival by billions and billions of living creatures. These creatures are busy trying to stay warm enough or cool enough, to eat enough other creatures, and avoid being eaten themselves. At the individual level this is generally a brutal and terrifying struggle.

Evolution is often summarised as the survival of the fittest, but the individuals which survive are not necessarily fitter than their competitors in the sense of being stronger or faster. They are more fit for their environment in the sense of being better adapted for it than the other creatures which are competing for the resources they need. Those which survive are able to pass on their genes, so the genes of the fittest creatures are passed on to subsequent generations, while the genes of individuals which were killed before reproducing are not passed on.

It is a common and understandable error to see evolution as a directed process which has been working diligently for billions of years to create the crowning pinnacle of nature – us. Evolution is not random: cause and effect is certainly present. But it is not trying to achieve a purpose, and it was not trying to create a conscious entity. In fact we don't even know whether consciousness arose because it conferred competitive advantage, or whether it was a by-product of something else which did. Just as we don't know why we walk on two legs rather than on all fours, or why we are the hairless ape, so we don't know how our consciousness arose. Did it precede language or follow it? Did it arise quickly or slowly?

Evolution is not a straight-line process either. It rarely – if ever— backtracks precisely, but it takes all sorts of circuitous, winding routes to get to any particular point. It is also very slow. It is true that creatures which are fantastically successful for millions of years can become extinct almost overnight – like the dinosaurs did when a huge asteroid hit Mexico and brought to a dramatic end their 160 million years as the dominant vertebrates. But change occurs mostly because of random mutations in the genes of parents, and the transition from one species to another typically takes many generations.

The fast, efficient way to develop a brain?

So the human brain is the result of a slow, ineffi-cient, un-directed process. Human scientists are now engaged in the project of creating artificial intelligence by a very different process, namely science. Science is purposeful and efficient: what works is built upon, and what fails is abandoned. If a slow and inefficient process can create a brain using nothing more than freely available organic chemicals, surely the much faster and more efficient process of science should be able to do the same.

Three reasons to be doubtful

Having looked at one argument for why it should be possible to create an artificial mind, let's turn to three arguments that have been advanced to prove that it will *not* be possible for us to create conscious machines. These are:

1. The Chinese Room thought experiment

2. The claim that consciousness involves quantum phenomena that cannot be replicated

3. The claim that we have souls

The Chinese Room

American philosopher John Searle first described his Chinese Room thought experiment in 1980. It tries to show that a computer which could engage in a conversation would not understand what it was doing, which means that it would not be conscious.

He described a computer that takes Chinese sentences as input, processes them by following the instructions of its software, and produces new sentences in Chinese as output. The software is so sophisticated that observers believe themselves to be engaged in conversation with a Chinese speaker.

Searle argued that this was the same as locking a person who does not speak Chinese inside a room with a version of the computer's software written out in English. Chinese speakers outside the room post pieces of paper into the room through a letterbox. The person inside the room processes them according to the instructions in the software and posts replies back to the outsiders. Once again the outsiders feel themselves to be engaged in conversation with a Chinese speaker, yet there is no Chinese speaker present.

Searle was not trying to prove that artificial intelligence could never appear to surpass humans in mental ability. He was also not denying that brains are machines: he is a materialist, believing that all phenomena, including consciousness, are the result of interactions between material objects and forces.

Rather he was arguing that computers do not process information in the way that human brains do. Until and unless one is built which does this, it will not be conscious, however convincing a simulation it produces.

Down the years Searle's argument has generated a substantial body of commentary, mostly claiming to refute it. Most computer scientists would say that the Chinese room is a very poor analogy for how a conscious machine would actually operate, and that a simple input-output device like this would not succeed in appearing to converse. Many have also claimed that if such a machine were to succeed, there *would* be an understanding of Chinese somewhere within the system – perhaps in the programme, or in the totality of the room, the person and the programme.

Quantum consciousness

The distinguished Oxford physicist Sir Roger Penrose argued in 1989 that human brains do not run the same kind of algorithms as computers. He claimed that a phenomenon described by quantum physics known as the wave function collapse could explain how consciousness arises. In 1992 he met an American anaesthetist called Dr Stuart Hammeroff, and the two collaborated on a theory of mind known as Orches-trated Objective Reduction (Orch-OR). It attributes consciousness to the behaviour of tiny components of cells called microtubules.

The two men have continued to develop their think-ing ever since, but the great majority of physicists and neuroscientists deny its plausibility. The main line of attack, articulated by US physicist Max Tegmark, is that collections of microtubules forming collapsing wave functions would be too small and act too quickly to have the claimed impact on the much larger scale of neurons.

Souls

Many religions, including notably the three great monotheistic religions of Christianity, Islam and Juda-ism, teach that humans are special because they have an immortal soul, implanted by their God. The soul is what gives rise to consciousness, and it is also what marks us as different from animals. The soul is a divine creation and cannot be replicated by humans.

As far as I know there is no scientific evidence for this claim, but according to no less a source than the CIA, over half the world's population are either Christian or Muslim.[30] On paper this looks like a serious problem for AGI research. Most people working on AGI are materialists, sceptical of the dualist claim that consciousness exists in a spiritual realm which is distinct and separate from the material one. This brings them into sharp intellectual conflict with the

(30) https://www.cia.gov/library/publications/the-world-factbook/geos/xx.html

teachings of these religions, which may indeed see them as blaspheming by seeking to usurp the prerogative of the almighty.

Fortunately, in practice many otherwise religious people take this claim about consciousness arising from an immaterial soul with a pinch of salt, in the same way as they turn a blind eye to their faith's injunction against contraception or alcohol, for instance. However, it is not hard to imagine that if and when the prospect of conscious machines comes closer, the research may come under fire from particularly ardent worshippers.

In the next three sections we will look at three ways to build a mind – an artificial system which can perform all the intellectual activities that an adult human can. They are:

1. Whole brain emulation

2. Building on artificial narrow intelligence

3. A comprehensive theory of mind

4.2 – Whole brain emulation

Whole brain emulation is the process of modelling (copying or replicating) the structures of a brain in very fine detail such that the model produces the same output as the original. So if a brain produces a mind, then the emulation (the model) produces a mind also. A replicated mind which is indistinguishable from the original is called an emulation. If the replicated mind is approximately the same, but differs in some important respects it is called a simulation.

Modelling a brain entails capturing the wiring diagram of the brain down a fine level of detail. The wiring diagram is called the connectome, by analogy with the genome, which is the map of an organism's genetic material.

Whole brain emulation is a mammoth undertaking. A human brain contains around 85 billion neurons (brain cells) and each neuron may have a thousand connections to other neurons. Imagine you could give every inhabitant of New York City a thousand pieces of string and tell them to hand the other end of each piece of string to a thousand other inhabitants, and have each piece of string send two hundred signals per second. Now multiply the city by a factor of ten thousand. That is a model of a human brain. It is often said to be the most complicated thing that we know of in the whole universe.

To make the job of brain emulation more complex, individual neurons – the cells which brains are made up of – are not simple beasts. They consist of a cell body, an axon to transmit signals to other neurons, and a number of dendrites to receive signals. Axons and dendrites pass signals to each other across gaps called synapses. The signals are conveyed to these gaps electrically, but the signal jumps across the gap by releasing neurotransmitters – chemical messengers. Axons can grow to as long as a metre in humans, with dendrites being much shorter.

As well as neurons, the brain is also stocked with glial cells. These were long thought to play a purely supporting role inside the brain: providing scaffolding for the neurons, insulating and sustaining them while they carry out the signalling work. Now it is known that glial cells do some of the signalling work themselves, and they also help neurons to form new connections.

The activity of neurons and glial cells is not binary, like microchips. They are not simply on or off. A neuron will fire a signal across its synapses according to how strongly and how frequently it is stimulated, and the strength and frequency of its own firing will vary as well. In a phenomenon known as synaptic plasticity, when two neurons communicate often enough their link becomes stronger and each becomes more likely to fire in response to the other.

It may seem an impossible task to scan and model a system with 85 billion components, especially when each component is complex itself. But there is no reason in principle why we cannot do it – as long as the brain is a purely physical entity, and our minds are not generated by some spiritual activity that lies beyond the grasp of scientific instruments. Is it feasible in practice?

We can break the problem down into three components: scanning, computational capacity, and modelling.

Scanning

Until very recently it seemed most likely that the first human brains to be comprehensively scanned will be cut into very thin slices and examined minutely with modern microscopic techniques. Scanners in general medical use today, such as MRI (Magnetic Resonance Imaging) are too blunt, resolving images in micrometres, which means one metre divided by a million. The resolution required for brain emulation is a thousand times greater, at the nano-metre level. (Atoms and molecules live at an even smaller scale, the pico-metre scale, which is a metre divided by a trillion, where a trillion is a one with twelve zeroes after it.)

Electron microscopes can generate images at the required resolution. Transmission electronic microscopy (TEM) sends electrons right through the target, while scanning electron microscopy (SEM) scatters electrons off its surface. Work has been going on for a decade on machines which scan brain matter at this scale quickly and accurately. One such device is the ATLUM, invented at Harvard University. It automatically slices a large volume of fixed brain tissue and mounts it on a continuous strip of very thin tape. The tape is then imaged in a scanning electron microscope.

Scanning a live brain rather than one which has been finely sliced will probably require sending tiny (molecular-scale) nano-robots into a brain to survey the neurons and glial cells and bring back sufficient data to create a 3D map. This is very advanced technology, but progress is surprisingly rapid.

There are also fascinating developments in light-sheet microscopy, where a microscope sends sheets of light (rather than a conventional electron beam) through the transparent brain of a larval zebra fish. The fish has been genetically modified so that its neurons make a protein that fluoresces in response to fluctuations in the concentration of calcium ions, which occur when nerve cells fire. A detector captures the signals and the system records activity from around 80% of the brain's 100,000 neurons every 1.3 seconds. [31]

So one way or another, the scanning looks achievable given technology that is available now, or soon will be.

Computational capacity

Computational capacity is the second challenge, and it is another big one. It is calculated that the human brain operates at the exaflop scale, meaning that it carries out one to the billion billion floating point operations per second – that is, one with eighteen zeroes after it. (A floating point operation is a calculation where the decimal point can be moved to the left or the right.)

Exascale computing is not just needed to model a human brain. It will also improve climate modelling, astronomy, ballistics analysis, engineering development and numerous other scientific, military and commercial endeavours. Major projects have been announced in many of the developed countries to achieve exascale computing before the end of this decade. President Obama's 2012 budget included a $126m fund to develop exascale computing, and Intel has set itself a deadline of 2018.

It therefore looks unlikely that computational capacity will long be an insuperable constraint on our ability to model a human brain. For some time after it arrives, exascale computing will be the preserve of very large, well-funded organisations. But assuming the processing power of computers continues to grow,

(31) http://www.nature.com/news/
flashing-fish-brains-filmed-in-action-1.12621

large organisations interested in brain emulation may be able to afford several such systems, and eventually even wealthy hobbyists will come into the market. This will certainly happen if Moore's Law continues (see next section), and will probably happen anyway if Moore's Law peters out, just at a slower pace.

Modelling

Imagine a future team of scientists has succeeded in scanning and recording the exact position of every neuron, glial cell, and other important components of a particular human brain. They have the computational and storage capacity to hold and manipulate the resulting data. They still have to identify the various components, fill in any gaps, work out how the components interact, and get the resulting model to carry out the same processes that the original brain did before they sliced it into tiny pieces. We don't yet know, but this may well turn out to be the hardest part of what is clearly a very hard overall project.

There is a prior example. For some years now, a complete connectome has been available of an organism called C. elegans. It is a tiny worm – just a millimetre long, and it lives in warm soils. It has the interesting property that almost all individuals of the species are hermaphrodite – just one in a thousand is male. C. elegans (Caenorhabditis elegans, in full) was one of the first multi-cellular organisms to have its genome mapped, and it was the first organism to have its connectome mapped – in outline back in 1986, and in more detail twenty years later. Not only mapped, but posted online in detail by the Open Worm project in May 2013.

C. elegans has a very small connectome compared to humans – just 302 neurons (compared to our 85 billion) and 7,000 synaptic connections. And yet it proved exceedingly hard to use the connectome of C. elegans to replicate its tiny mind. Some researchers poured cold water on the idea that having a connectome could enable a creature's mind to be replicated. One analogy was that the connectome is like a road map, but it tells you nothing about how many cars use the road, what type of car, and where they all go.

However, a breakthrough was achieved in December 2013 when researchers were able to make a model of the worm wriggle. Then in November 2014, a team led by one of the founders of the Open Worm project used the C. elegans connectome to control a small wheeled robot made out of Lego. The robot displayed worm-like behaviour despite having had no programming apart from what was contained in the connectome.

The Human Brain Project (HBP) and Obama's BRAIN initiative

Henry Markram, an Israeli / South African neuroscientist, has become a controversial figure in his field while attracting enormous funding for projects to reverse engineer the human brain. In an influential TED talk, he suggested that an accurate model of the brain could enable scientists to devise cures for the diseases which afflict it, such as Alzheimer's disease. As people live longer, more of us succumb to brain diseases, which can ruin our final years. He does not tend to talk about creating a conscious mind *in silico,* although he did tell a Guardian journalist in 2007 that "if we build [the model] right, it should speak."[32]

In 2005 he launched the Blue Brain project, based at Lausanne in Switzerland. Its initial goal was to model the 10,000 neurons and 30 million synapses in the neocortical column of a rat. The neocortex is a series of layers at the surface of the brain which are involved in our higher mental functions, such as conscious thought and our use of language. A neocortical column is the smallest functional unit within the neocortex, and is around 2mm tall and 0.5mm wide. (Human neocortical columns have 60,000 neurons each, and we have a thousand times more of them than a rat. A rat's brain has 200 million neurons altogether, compared with the 85 billion in a human brain.)

In November 2007 Markram announced that the model of the rat's neorcortical column was complete, and its circuits responded to input stimuli in the same way as its organic counterpart.

Markram went on to raise the impressive sum of €1.2 billion for the Human Brain Project, also based in Lausanne. Most of the funding came from the European Union, but the project involves researchers from over a hundred organisations in 26 countries. It is organised into 13 sub-projects, and its overall goals are to better organise the world's neuroscience knowledge, to improve the computer capabilities available to neuroscientists, and to build "working models" of first a

(32) http://www.theguardian.com/technology/2007/dec/20/research.it

rat brain and then a human brain. The principal use of these models, according to HBP pronouncements, will be to understand how brain diseases work and to greatly improve the way therapies are developed and tested.

The Human Brain Project is controversial in neuroscientific circles, with critics subjecting it to the kind of vitriol which academics excel at. Some worry that its massive funding will drain resources away from alternative projects, which suggests they believe that scientific funding is a zero-sum game. Others argue that our limited understanding of how the brain works means that the attempt to model it is premature. In July 2014, 200 neuroscientists signed a letter calling for a review of the way the project distributes its funding.

One of the Human Brain Project's harshest critics is Facebook's Yann LeCun, who said in February 2015 that "a big chunk of the Human Brain Project in Europe is based on the idea that we should build chips that reproduce the functioning of neurons as closely as possible, and then use them to build a gigantic computer, and somehow when we turn it on with some learning rule, AI will emerge. I think it's nuts."

President Obama announced the BRAIN initiative (Brain Research through Advancing Innovative Neurotechnologies – a backronym if ever there was one) in April 2013. It is likely to spend $300m a year over the decade it is projected to run for. It has proved less controversial than the HBP because its funding is being dispensed by three federal organisations, and it is at pains to involve a wide range of research organisations. There are concerted attempts to co-ordinate the BRAIN project and the HBP to avoid unnecessary duplication, and make sure that each project feeds into the other productively. At the risk of over-simplifying, the BRAIN project is funding the development of tools and methodologies, and the HBP is building the actual model of a brain.

Reasons why whole brain emulation might not work

The more detailed a model has to be, the harder it is to build. If a brain's functions can be replicated to an acceptable level by modelling just the cortical columns, the process will happen fairly quickly. More likely, the model will have to capture data about the configuration of individual neurons in order to function adequately, and obviously that is a much harder task. But if that is not enough, and the layout of each dendrite and other cellular component needs to be replicated accurately, the task becomes more difficult by orders of magnitude. In the worst case, it would not be possible to produce a working model without specifying the layouts of individual molecules – or even sub-atomic quantum particles. If that level of granularity is required, the project might be impossible – at least for several centuries.

Granularity is one potential source of difficulty. Time is another. The modelling techniques being developed today can capture the relative positions of neurons and other brain material, and their connectivity with each other. If non-destructive scanning techniques remain limited in scope, we may not be able to record the behaviour over time of each individual component that needs to be modelled. Yet we know that neurons behave in complex ways, and that their behaviour is strongly affected by their interaction. Perhaps the models being constructed now will prove uninformative because they lack this time series data.

What happens when you run a model which lacks sufficient granularity and lacks time series data? Usually an approximately accurate model generates approximately accurate results. But approximately accurate may in some cases be so far off the mark as to be positively misleading and counter-productive. Henry Markram claims that his simulated neocortical column of a rat produced responses very similar to the biological original. We won't know how accurate the whole brain models will be until they are tested – if then.

Perhaps there is a spectrum of reproduceability. Imagine that you could capture exact data about the brain components down to the sub-atomic level over an extended period of time. It is reasonable to think that would enable you to produce a copy of a brain which would generate a mind indistinguishable from the original: it would perceive, respond and reason in exactly the same way as the person whose brain was copied. (Let's not get into the philosophical discussion here of whether it would be the same person, or a new person who was a copy of the original.)

Perhaps a less accurate model, where the data was less detailed or the time series was shorter, would generate the mind of a rather different person. And perhaps a model based on significantly inaccurate data would generate gibberish, or inhuman behaviours.

Over the next few decades we may resolve some of these questions.

4.3 – Building on narrow AI

Symbolic AI

When AI got started in the 1950s it tried to reduce human thought to the manipulation of symbols, such as language and maths, which could be made comprehensible to computers. This is known as symbolic AI, or Good Old-Fashioned AI (GOFAI). Its most successful results were the expert systems which flourished in the late 1980s. It soon became apparent that there were diminishing returns to investment in these systems, and when the second AI winter thawed in the early 1990s it was thanks to the rise of more statistical approaches, which are often collectively termed machine learning.

Machine Learning

Machine learning is the process of creating and refining algorithms which can produce conclusions based on data without being explicitly programmed to do so. It overlaps closely with a number of other domains, including pattern recognition: machine learning algorithms are becoming increasingly impressive at recognising images, for instance. Another is computational statistics, which is the development of algorithms to implement statistical methods on computers. A third is the field of data mining, and its offshoot Big Data.

Data mining is the process of discovering previously unknown properties in large data sets, whereas machine learning systems usually make predictions based on information which is already known to the experimenter, using training data.

For instance, when training a machine to recognise faces, or images of cats, the researchers will present the machine with thousands of images and the machine will devise statistical rules for categorising images based on their common features. Then the machine is presented with another set of images to see whether the rules hold up, or need revising.

Machine learning has proven to be a powerful tool, with impressive performance in applications like computer vision and search. One of the most promising approaches to computer vision at the moment is "convolutional neural nets", in which a large number of artificial neurons are each assigned to a tiny portion of an image. It is an interesting microcosm of the whole field of machine learning in that it was first invented in 1980, but did not become really useful until the 21st century when graphics processing unit (GPU) computer chips enabled researchers to assemble very large networks.

Rather than overtly seeking to build a conscious mind, most practitioners are seeking to emulate particular intellectual skills at which humans have traditionally beaten computers. There are notable exceptions, such as Doug Lenart, whose Cyc project has been trying to emulate common sense since 1984, and Ben Goertzel, whose OpenCog project is attempting to build an open source artificial general intelligence system.

The learning that a machine learning computer system does can be supervised or unsupervised. If supervised, the computer is given both inputs and outputs by the researcher, and required to work out the rules that connect them. If unsupervised, the machine is given no pointers, and has to identify the inputs and the outputs as well as the rules that connect them. A special case is reinforcement learning, where the computer gets feedback from the environment – for instance by playing a video game.

Statistical techniques

Machine learning employs a host of clever statistical techniques. Two of the most commonly cited are "Bayesian networks", and "Hidden Markov Models", which have achieved almost sacred status in AI research circles.

A Bayesian network is a graphical structure that allows you to make hypotheses about uncertain situations. The system generates a flow chart with arrows linking a number of boxes, each of which contains a variable or an event. It assigns probabilities to each of them happening, dependant on what happens with each of the other variables. The variables might be, for instance, missing the last train, spending a night in the open, catching pneumonia, and dying. The system would test the accuracy of the linkages and the probabilities by running large sets of actual data through the model, and end up (hopefully) with a reliably predictive model.

Andrej Markov was a Russian mathematician who died in 1922 and in the type of model that bears his name the next step depends only on the current step, and not any previous steps. A Hidden Markov Model (often abbreviated to HMM because they are so useful) is one where the current state is only partially observable. They are particularly useful in speech recognition and handwriting recognition systems.

Deep learning

Deep learning is a subset of machine learning. Its algorithms use several layers of processing, each taking data from previous layers and passing an output up to the next layer. The nature of the output may vary according to the nature of the input, which is not necessarily binary, just on or off, but can be weighted. The number of layers can vary too, with anything above ten layers seen as very deep learning.

Artificial neural nets (ANN) are an important type of deep learning system – indeed some people argue that deep learning is simply a re-branding of neural networks. The first experiments with ANNs were made in the 1950s, and Frank Rosenblatt used them to construct the Mark I Perceptron, the first computer which could learn new skills by trial and error. Early hopes for the quick development of thinking machines were dashed, however, and neural nets fell into disuse until the late 1980s, when they experienced a renaissance along with what came to be known as deep learning thanks to pioneers Yann LeCun (now at Facebook),

Geoff Hinton (now at Google) and Yoshua Bengio, a professor at the University of Montreal.

Yann LeCun describes deep learning as follows. "A pattern recognition system is like a black box with a camera at one end, a green light and a red light on top, and a whole bunch of knobs on the front. The learning algorithm tries to adjust the knobs so that when, say, a dog is in front of the camera, the red light turns on, and when a car is put in front of the camera, the green light turns on. You show a dog to the machine. If the red light is bright, don't do anything. If it's dim, tweak the knobs so that the light gets brighter. If the green light turns on, tweak the knobs so that it gets dimmer. Then show a car, and tweak the knobs so that the red light gets dimmer and the green light gets brighter. If you show many examples of the cars and dogs, and you keep adjusting the knobs just a little bit each time, eventually the machine will get the right answer every time.

"Now, imagine a box with 500 million knobs, 1,000 light bulbs, and 10 million images to train it with. That's what a typical Deep Learning system is."

Games

We noted in chapter 1 that games have an advantage as test and development environments for machine learning because they don't involve the tricky engineering required by physical robots. Since 2005 a group at Stanford University has hosted the International General Game Playing Competition, which offers a $10,000 prize to the winning machine. The contestants cannot run specialised software designed specifically for a particular game, as they are only given the rules shortly before play begins. In the first competition, humans were able to beat the best machines, but that has not happened since.

The first generation of game-playing software, back in 2005, did not plan ahead; instead they selected moves which maximised the current position. The second generation, from 2007, employed the sort of statistical methods discussed above, and in particular the Monte Carlo search technique which plays out large numbers of randomly selected moves and compares the final outcomes. The third generation machines currently winning the competition allocate more resources to learning about the game during the short preparation period in order to devise optimal playing strategies.

A machine called Cepheus was announced in early 2015 to be unbeatable at two-person Texas limit hold'em poker, which is significant because it is a game in which the players have imperfect information. (In no-limit hold'em poker, where you can raise the bet by any amount, people are still beating computers – although only just.)

Building a brain with traditional AI

It is a common but controversial observation that systems using these techniques seem to operate in similar ways to the internal workings of parts of the human brain. Your brain is not like a car, a single system whose component units all work together in a clearly structured way which is constant over time, and all co-ordinated by a controlling entity (the driver). It is more like a vast array of disparate systems using hardware components (neurons) that are scattered all over its volume, seemingly at random. We don't know exactly how consciousness emerges from this interplay of huge numbers of circuits firing, but it does seem that you need a lot of them to be firing away simultaneously to generate waking consciousness. (The old chestnut that you only use 10% of your brain's capacity is a – discredited myth.)

The speculation that a system containing enough of the types of operations involved in machine learning might generate a conscious mind intrigues some neuroscientists, and strikes others as wildly implausible, or as something that is many years away. Gary Marcus, a psychology professor at New York University, says "deep learning is only part of the larger challenge of building intelligent machines. Such techniques [are] still a long way from integrating abstract knowledge, such as information about what objects are, what they are for, and how they are typically used. The most powerful A.I. systems, like Watson, . . . use techniques like deep learning as just one element in a very complicated ensemble of techniques . . ."[33]

Andrew Ng, formerly head of the Google Brain project and now in charge of Baidu's AI activities, says that current machine learning techniques are like a "cartoon version" of the human brain. Yann LeCun is also cautious: "My least favourite description is, 'It works just like the brain.' I don't like people saying this

(33) http://www.newyorker.com/news/news-desk/
is-deep-learning-a-revolution-in-artificial-intelligence

because, while deep learning gets an inspiration from biology, it's very, very far from what the brain actually does. And describing it like the brain gives a bit of the aura of magic to it, which is dangerous. It leads to hype; people claim things that are not true. AI has gone through a number of AI winters because people claimed things they couldn't deliver."

Computational neuroscientist Dr Dan Goodman of Imperial College, London offers a good illustration of how different deep learning is from the way the brain works: to teach a computer to recognise a lion you have to show it millions of pictures of different lions in different poses. A human only needs to see a few such pictures. We are able to learn about categories of items at a higher level of abstraction. AGI optimists think that we will work out how to do that with computers too.

There are plenty of serious AI researchers who do believe that the probabilistic techniques of machine learning will lead to AGI within a few decades rather than centuries. The veteran AI researcher Geoff Hinton, now working at Google, forecast in May 2015 that the first machine with common sense could be developed in ten years. [34]

Part of the reason for the difference of opinion may be that the latter group take very seriously the notion that exponential progress in computing capability will speed progress towards the creation of an AGI. We will discuss this in the next chapter.

If the first AGI is created using systems like the ones

(34) http://www.theguardian.com/science/2015/may/21/
google-a-step-closer-to-developing-machines-with-human-like-intelligence

described above it is likely that it would be significantly different from a human brain, both in operation and in behaviour. While a successful whole brain emulation could be expected to produce something which thought somewhat like a human, an AGI based on traditional AI might think in an entirely alien way.

4.4 – A comprehensive theory of mind

The third approach to building an artificial general intelligence is to develop a comprehensive theory of mind – that is, to achieve a complete understanding of how the mind works – and to use that knowledge to build an artificial one. Although neuroscience has probably made more progress in the last 20 years than in the whole of human history beforehand, we are still very far from a complete theory of mind. If no serious attempt was made to build an AGI until such a theory was complete it would probably not happen until well past the end of this century.

Most AI researchers would argue this is to make the task unnecessarily difficult. Humans have probably looked longingly up at the sky and envied birds their power of flight ever since they became able to think in such terms. Down the ages, men have tried to fly by copying what birds do, but when we finally did learn to fly, it was not by copying birds. There are still things we don't understand about how birds fly, yet we can now fly further and faster that they can.

AI may be the same. The first AGI may be the result of whole brain emulation, backed up by only a partial understanding of exactly how all the neurons and other cells in any particular human brain fit together and work. Or it may be an assemblage of many thousands of deep learning systems, creating a form of intelligence quite different from our own, and operating in a way we don't understand – at least initially. Many AI researchers would argue that it will be easier to understand the fine details of how a human brain works by building and understanding an artificial one than the other way around.

4.5 – Conclusion: can we build a brain?

The bottom line is that we don't know for certain whether we can build a brain, or a conscious machine. But the existence of our own brains, producing rich conscious lives (or so we believe) in seven billion humans around the world, is proof that consciousness can be generated by a material entity – unless you believe in a dualist soul, or something similar. Evolution, although powerful, is slow and inefficient, and science is relatively fast and efficient, so in principle we should be able to build a brain.

The eminent AI researcher Christof Koch, chief scientific officer of the Allen Institute for Brain Science in Seattle, has long been sceptical of AGI being created soon. But he does accept that "if you were to build a computer that has the same circuitry as the brain, this computer would also have consciousness associated with it." In recent interviews he has suggested that AGI might arrive in the next 50 years. [35]

Very few neuroscientists argue that it will *never* be possible to create conscious machines. A few scientists, like Roger Penrose, think there is something ineffable about human thought which means it could not be recreated in silicon. This type of extreme scepticism about the AGI field is rare.

So the debate today is not so much about whether we can create an AGI, but when. It is this question that we will address next.

(35). https://intelligence.org/2014/05/13/
christof-koch-stuart-russell-machine-superintelligence

CHAPTER 5
WHEN MIGHT AGI ARRIVE?

5.1 – Expert opinion

Some people think it will be soon

Elon Musk has made a name for himself as a Cassandra about AI, with remarks about working on AGI being akin to summoning the demon, and how humans might turn out to be just the boot loader (startup system) for digital superintelligence. Not only does he see AGI as an existential threat to humanity: he also thinks the danger will manifest soon. In a post at Edge.com[36] which was subsequently deleted, he said "The pace of progress in artificial intelligence (I'm not referring to narrow AI) is incredibly fast. Unless you have direct exposure to groups like Deepmind, you have no idea how fast – it is growing at a pace close to exponential. The risk of something seriously dangerous happening is in the five year timeframe. 10 years at

(36) http://uk.businessinsider.com/elon-musk-killer-robots-will-be-here-with-in-five-years-2014-11#ixzz3XHt6A8Lt

most. This is not a case of crying wolf about something I don't understand."

Demis Hassabis, founder of the company Musk was referring to responded by downplaying the immediacy of the threat: "We agree with him there are risks that need to be borne in mind, but we're decades away from any sort of technology that we need to worry about,"

Whatever you think of Musk's warnings, he has at least put his money where his mouth is. He invests in companies like DeepMind and Vicarious, another AI pioneer, in order to keep up to speed with their progress. And he has donated $10 million to the Future of Life Institute, one of the organisations looking for ways to make the arrival of AGI safe.

However genuine and well-informed Musk's fears are, there are plenty of people who remain sceptical.

The future isn't what it used to be

We are curiously nostalgic about the future. People point out that technologies which futurists confidently expected several decades ago have yet to materialise: "where's my jetpack?" is a common refrain. When 2015 rolled around, people celebrated the fact that this was the year depicted in *Back to the Future*, the biggest movie of 1985, by asking, "hey dude, where's my hoverboard?"

PayPal founder Peter Thiel laments the slower-than-expected progress by saying that "we were promised flying cars and instead what we got was 140 characters" (ie, Twitter).

Yet we also got the ability to access almost every

fact, idea or thought that a human has ever recorded within a couple of seconds, which people 100 years ago would probably have viewed as far more impressive than flying cars. It is amazing how quickly we humans become habituated to the marvels we create, and simply take them for granted. We will look at this again later in this chapter.

Similarly, some people are dismissive of the progress made by artificial intelligence since the discipline began 60 years ago, complaining that we don't yet have a machine which knows it is alive. But it is daft to dismiss as failures today's best pattern recognition systems, self-driving cars, and machines which can beat any human at many games of skill.

Informed scepticism about near-term AGI

We should take more seriously the arguments of very experienced AI researchers who claim that although the AGI undertaking is possible, it won't be achieved for a very long time. Rodney Brooks, a veteran AI researcher and robot builder, says "I think it is a mistake to be worrying about us developing [strong] AI any time in the next few hundred years. I think the worry stems from a fundamental error in not distinguishing the difference between the very real recent advances in a particular aspect of AI, and the enormity and complexity of building sentient volitional intelligence."

Andrew Ng at Baidu and Yann LeCun at Facebook are of a similar mind, as we saw in the last chapter.

Less sceptical experts

However there are also plenty of veteran AI researchers who think AGI may arrive soon. Stuart Russell is a British computer scientist and AI researcher who is, along with Peter Norvig, a director of research at Google, co-author of one of the field's standard university textbooks, "Artificial Intelligence: A Modern Approach". Russell was one of the co-authors of the Huffington Post article in April 2014 which propelled Stephen Hawking into the limelight as a leading proponent of the idea that much more work is needed to ensure that AGI is friendly toward humans.

Nils Nilsson is one of the founders of the science of artificial intelligence, and has been on the faculty of Stanford's Computer Science department since 1985. He was a founding fellow of the Association for the Advancement of Artificial Intelligence (AAAI), and its fourth president. In 2012 he estimated the chance of AGI arriving by 2050 as 50%.

When I asked another veteran AI researcher in March 2015 why the grandees mentioned above are so confident that AGI is centuries away rather than decades, he replied that they don't have crystal balls. His own estimate was the late 2020s. He added that many AI researchers are fearful of the backlash that could result if the general public became aware of the possibility that AGI could be created in a couple of decades, and what the implications could be. They are probably right to be concerned.

Nick Bostrom's meta-survey

For his 2014 book *"Superintelligence"*, Nick Bostrom compiled four recent surveys of AI experts, which asked for estimates of the dates at which the probability of AGI being created reached 10%, 50% and 90%. The surveys were carried out in 2012 and 2013. It is unclear how many of the respondents were scientists actively engaged in AI research as opposed to philosophers and theoreticians, but all were either highly-cited authors of published academic work on AI, or professional academics attending conferences on the subject.

The combined estimates were as follows: 10% probability of AGI arriving by 2022, 50% chance by 2040 and 90% chance by 2075. Bostrom himself thinks the upper bound is over-optimistic, but the median estimate is in line with other opinion surveys. He cautions that these are of course just estimates, albeit as well-informed as any. [37]

5.2 – Moore's Law and exponential growth

Moore's Law

One reason sometimes given for the wide range of opinions about the likely arrival time of AGI is that it is likely to be strongly affected by the continuation or otherwise of the exponential growth in computer processing power known as Moore's Law. Most people struggle to comprehend the impact of exponential growth, and many of those who do comprehend it

(37) I am grateful to Russell Buckley for drawing my attention to this illustration.

doubt that Moore's Law will continue much longer.

Gordon Moore is one of the founders of Intel, the world's largest manufacturer of computer chips. In 1965 Moore observed that his company was cramming twice as many transistors on each chip every two years. The observation was subsequently re-framed as a "law", refined to a period of 18 months, and broadened to mean that the processing power of $1,000-worth of computer was doubling every period.

Moore's Law celebrated its 50th anniversary in April 2015. Given its importance in human affairs there was remarkably little fanfare.

Exponential growth

Doubling something every period is exponential growth, and exponential growth turns out to be astonishingly fast. If you take thirty steps ahead you will travel about thirty yards. If you could double the length of your stride with each step you would reach the moon – and back again. It takes most people quite a while to get their heads around this.

Another un-intuitive feature of exponential growth is that the change is concentrated at the end of the period of time under review. Imagine you are in a football stadium which has been made waterproof. Someone places a single drop of water on the pitch. Sixty seconds later they place two drops there, and another sixty seconds later they place four drops – and so on, exponentially. How long do you think it would take to drown the people in the top row of seats? The surprising answer is 49 minutes. What is more, after

45 minutes the stadium is 93% empty of water – a spectator would just about be able to see the liquid covering the pitch. The vast majority of the water arrives in the last four minutes.

People often talk about the "knee" of an exponential curve, the point at which past progress seems sluggish, and projected future growth looks dramatic. This is a misapprehension. When you compare exponential curves plotted for ten and 100 periods of the same growth, they look pretty much the same. In other words, wherever you are on the curve, the past always looks horizontal and the future always looks vertical. We may think we have had rapid progress to bring us today's smartphones, but really it was nothing compared to the progress we will see in the future – if Moore's Law holds.

Exponential curves do not generally last for long: they are just too powerful. In most contexts, fast-growing phenomena start off slowly, pick up speed to an exponential rate, and then after a few periods they tail off to form an S-shaped curve. This is as true of the population growth in animal species as it is of the life cycle of products and services.

However we have plenty of examples of exponentials continuing for many steps, and in fact each of us is one of them. Each of us is composed of around 27 trillion cells, which were created by fission – an exponential process. It required 46 steps of fission to create all of your 27 trillion cells. Moore's Law, by comparison, has had 33 steps in the 50 years of its existence.

People have been claiming for years that Moore's

Law is tailing off – or even that it has stopped. But Moore's Law has proved surprisingly robust. Ray Kurzweil claims it has been in force since before integrated circuits came along, stretching back into the ancient history of vacuum tubes and beyond.

And it looks as though there is life in the old law yet. In February 2015 Intel updated journalists on their chip programme for the next few years, and it maintains the exponential growth. [38] The first chips based on its new 10 nanometre manufacturing process are expected in late 2016 / early 2017, after which it expects to move away from silicon, probably towards a III-V semiconductor such as indium gallium arsenide. [39]

Exascale computing

Moore's Law is important to questions about AGI because computer processing power enables many of the processes which in turn could enable AGI. In the last chapter we saw how whole brain emulation requires continued improvements in scanning, computational capacity, and modelling. Each of these requires faster and more powerful computers. Similarly, narrow AI techniques are improving all the time as faster and more powerful computers become available.

One of the milestones anticipated by AI researchers is the availability of exascale computing. We saw in the last chapter that the brain operates at the exaflop scale,

(38) http://arstechnica.com/gadgets/2015/02/
intel-forges-ahead-to-10nm-will-move-away-from-silicon-at-7nm/

(39) The "III-V" refers to the periodic table group the material belongs to. Transistors made from these semiconductors should consume far less power, and also switch much faster.

carrying out ten to the eighteenth power floating point operations per second. Nobody is suggesting that when the first supercomputer operates at the exascale level it will suddenly wake up and start thinking like a human brain. If consciousness arose because of a sheer mass of information processing, the internet would have woken up by now. But reaching that threshold will be a significant step as well as a remarkable achievement.

One of the first systems to operate at the exascale may be the Square Kilometer Array telescope system. Headquartered in the UK and using a co-ordinated array of radio telescopes located in remote areas of Australia and South Africa, the system is scheduled to start construction in 2018 and start scanning the sky in the early 2020s. It is reported that once it is fully operational it will generate half as much data as is transferred across the entire internet today. That in itself is a striking example of the power of exponential growth.

Why don't we notice the exponential rate of improvement in AI?

Most of the things which are of vital interest to us change at a linear rate. Leopards chase us and our prey eludes us one step at a time; the seasons change one day at a time. We have a hard time adjusting to things that change at an exponential rate. But even when it is pointed out to us we often choose to ignore it. Here are seven possible reasons why many people shrug off the extraordinary progress of AI as not significant.

1. Back in chapter 1 we encountered Tesler's

Theorem, in which AI is defined as "whatever hasn't been done yet". It is easy to dismiss AI as not progressing very fast if you allocate all its achievements to some other domain.

2. The demise of Moore's Law has been predicted ever since it was devised fifty years ago. There is no need to worry about a phenomenon which is almost over.

3. We noted earlier in this chapter that we are curiously nostalgic about the future that we once thought we would have. We haven't got hover boards, flying cars or personal jetpacks, but we have got pretty close to omniscience at the touch of a button. What's coming next is no less amazing, but we tend to focus on what we didn't get more than what we did.

4. Adoption is getting quicker but penetration isn't. It is often claimed that each new technology takes less time than any of its predecessors to achieve mass adoption. In fact this is not true. It is true that Facebook was adopted faster by the first million people (and then the first hundred million) than the internet was, which in turn was adopted by that number faster than TV was, and so on. But TV was adopted by 50% and then 75% of the population at pretty much the same speed as the internet and then Facebook. The difference is that the population has grown significantly since TV was launched. It may be

that people have a subliminal understanding of this, and it renders them less impressed by the hype about each new invention.

5. Another aspect of the hype around each new invention is that their early incarnations are often disappointing. If you were around for the launch of the first mobile phones you will remember they were a bit of a joke: the size of a brick and the weight of a small suitcase, they were ridiculed as the expensive playthings of pretentious yuppies. Now almost everyone in the developed world has a smartphone. Similar ridicule attended the launch of Siri and Google Glass, but contrary to popular opinion, they are emphatically not failures. They are simply the first, tentative outings of technologies which will soon revolutionise our lives.

    Less fuss has so far been made about another extraordinary innovation: an app called Crystal trawls the internet for anything written by a person of interest to you and helps you draft your communication with them. It is in beta mode at the time of writing, and many of those who have tried it have criticised it as both creepy and ineffective. They are forgetting the often-repeated lesson: this technology will improve, and its contribution to our productivity and our effectiveness will be substantial.

    In fact these technologies are simply following the standard curve of the product life cycle. At the initial launch of a new product a small tribe of what marketers call "innovators" jump on it because it is new and shiny. They can see its potential and they generate some early hype. The "early adopters" then try it out and declare it not fit for purpose – and they are right. The backlash sets in, and a wave of cynicism submerges all interest in the product. Over successive months or years the technology gradually improves, and eventually crosses a threshold at which point it is fit for purpose. In technology marketing circles this is known as crossing the chasm, and of course many technologies never manage it. They never find their killer application.

Those technologies which do cross the chasm are then adopted by the "early majority", then the "late majority", and finally by the "laggards". But by the time the early majority is getting on board the hype is already ancient history, and people are already taking for granted the improvement to their lives. The hype cycle has run its course.

6. The hedonic treadmill is a name for the fact that most people have a fairly constant level of happiness (hedonic level), and that when something significant in our life changes – for good or bad – we quickly adjust and return to our previous level. When we look ahead to an anticipated event we often believe that it will

change our lives permanently, and that we will feel happier – or less happy – forever afterwards. When the event actually happens we quickly become accustomed to the new reality, and what seemed wonderful in prospects becomes ordinary. "Wow" quickly becomes "meh".

7. Learning about a new AI breakthrough is slightly unsettling for many people. There is a vague awareness that we may be creating our own competition, and of course there is the image of the Terminator, which has been entertaining us frightfully for over 30 years. At a deep level, many of us really don't want to acknowledge the exponential rate of AI improvement.

5.3 – Unpredictable breakthroughs

Professor Russell doesn't have much time for predictions based on Moore's Law, and he is dismissive of attempts to equate the processing power of computers and animals. He thinks AGI will arrive not because of the exponential improvement in computer performance, but because researchers will come up with new paradigms; new ways of thinking about problem-solving. He doesn't claim to know how many new paradigms will be required or when they will arrive. His best guess is that they may be a few decades away. If he is right, we may get little or no warning of the arrival of the first AGI, and it is therefore all the more urgent that we start work on the challenge of ensuring that the first superintelligence is beneficial. We will explore that challenge in part four.

5.4 – Conclusion

Expert opinion is divided about when the first AGI might be created. Some think it could be less than a decade, others are convinced it is centuries away. One thing that is clear, though, is that the belief that AGI could arrive within a few decades is not the preserve of a few crackpots. Sober and very experienced scientists think so too. It is a possibility we should take seriously.

Creating an AGI is very hard. But serious consideration of exponential growth makes very hard problems seem more tractable. Buckminster Fuller estimated that at the start of the twentieth century the sum of human knowledge was doubling every century, and that by the end of the second world war that had reduced to twenty-five years.[40] Now it takes 13 months and in 2006 IBM estimated that when the internet of things becomes a reality the rate would be every 12 hours.[41]

The football stadium thought experiment illustrates how progress at exponential rate can take you by surprise – even when you are looking for it. Many sensible people become suspicious when they hear the phrase exponential growth: they fear it used as a cover for wishful (or so-called "magical") thinking. Others question how long Moore's Law can continue. Their scepticism is healthy, but it doesn't change the

(40) http://www.industrytap.com/
knowledge-doubling-every-12-months-soon-to-be-every-12-hours/3950

(41) http://www-935.ibm.com/services/no/cio/leverage/levinfo_wp_gts_
thetoxic.pdf

facts. Many serious experts think that AGI could be with us this century, and if Moore's Law continues for another decade or so then very dramatic developments are possible.

PART THREE: ASI

Artificial Superintelligence

CHAPTER 6
WILL ARTIFICIAL GENERAL INTELLIGENCE LEAD TO SUPERINTELLIGENCE?

Artificial superintelligence (ASI) is generally known simply as superintelligence. It does not need the prefix artificial since there is no natural predecessor.

6.1 – What is superintelligence?

How smart are we?

We have no idea of how much smarter than us it is possible to be. It might be that for some reason humans are near the limit of how intelligent a creature can become, but it seems very unlikely. We have good reason to believe that overall, we are the smartest species on this planet at the moment, and we have achieved great things. As a result, the future of all the other species on Earth depends largely on our decisions and actions. Yet we have already been overtaken – and by a very long way – by our own creations in various limited aspects of intelligence. Humble pocket calculators can execute arithmetic processes far faster and more reliably than we can. Granted they cannot walk around or enjoy a sunset, but they are smarter than us in their specific domain. Likewise chess computers, and self-driving cars.

More generally, we humans are subject to a range of cognitive biases which mar our otherwise impressive intelligence. "Inattentional blindness" can render us surprisingly dim-witted on occasion, as demonstrated by the selective attention test, which involves watching an informal game of basketball. (If you haven't seen it before you can take the test here: http://bit.ly/1gX-mThe – it's fun.) The flip side of this is "salience", when something you have reason to pay attention to starts appearing everywhere you look. Thus if you buy a Lexus car, there may suddenly seem to be many more of them on the road than before.

"Anchoring" is another way in which we are easily misled. If you ask people whether Mahatma Gandhi was older than 35 when he died and then ask them to guess his exact age when he died, they will give a lower answer than if your first question was whether he was over 100 when he died. (To save you looking it up, he was 78.)

Some of our forms of bias are very damaging. How much better would our political processes be if we were not subject to "confirmation bias", which makes us more attentive to data and ideas which confirm our existing viewpoints than to data and ideas which challenge them?

So it is easy to imagine that there could be minds much smarter than ours. They could hold more facts and ideas in their heads (if they had heads) at one time. They could work their way through mathematical calculations and logical arguments faster and more reliably. They could be free of the biases and distortions which plague our thinking.

In fact there is no good reason to suppose that we are anywhere near the upper limit of the intelligence spectrum – if there is such a limit. It may very well be that there could be beings with intelligence as far ahead of ours as ours is ahead of an ant. Perhaps there are such beings somewhere in the universe right now, in which case the fascinating Fermi Paradox asks why we see no evidence of them.

And perhaps we are on the way to creating one.

Consciousness

There is no need to pre-judge whether a superintelligence would be conscious or self-aware. It is logically possible that a mind could have volition, and be greatly more effective than humans at solving all problems based on information it could learn, without having the faintest notion that it was doing so. As mentioned in chapter 1, it is hard for us to comprehend how a mind could have all the cognitive ability that a normal adult human has without being conscious, but logical possibility isn't constrained by the limitations of our imaginations.

6.2 – How to be smarter

Broadly speaking, there are three ways that an AGI could have its intelligence enhanced. Its mind could be faster, bigger, or have better architecture.

Faster

If the first AGI is a brain emulation it might well start out running at the same speed as the human brain it was modelled on. The fastest speed that signals travel within neurons is around 100 metres per second. Signals travel between neurons at junctions called synapses, where the axon (the longest part of a neuron) of one neuron meets the dendrite of another one. This crossing takes the form of chemicals jumping across the gap, which is why neuron signalling is described as an electro-chemical process. The synapse jumping part is much slower than the electrical part.

Signals within computers typically travel at 200 *million* metres per second – well over half the speed of light. So by using the faster signalling speeds available to computers than to brains, a brain emulation AGI could operate 2 million times faster than a human.

It is interesting to speculate whether this AGI, if conscious, would experience life at 2 million times the speed of a human. If so it would find waiting around for us to do something very boring. It would experience events that happen too quickly for us to be able to follow them – such as explosions – as slow and manageable processes. Or perhaps the subjective experience of time is consistent across minds, and the super-fast AGI would simply be able to fit a lot more thinking than we can into any given period.

Bigger

We do not yet know what kind of computer technology will generate the first AGI. It may use neuromorphic chips (which mimic aspects of the way the brain operates), or even quantum computing (which makes use of spooky quantum phenomena like entanglement and superposition). One thing that is true of all the types of computers we know about so far is that you can make them more powerful by adding more hardware.

Modern supercomputers are made up of large numbers of servers. At the time of writing, the fastest supercomputer in the world is China's Tianhe-2, which has 32,000 CPUs in 125 cabinets. [42] Memory can also be expanded simply by plugging in more hardware.

Once the first AGI is created, its intelligence could be expanded by adding extra hardware in a way that is sadly impossible for human brains.

Better architecture

Although humans are the most intelligent species on Earth, we do not have the biggest brains. That honour belongs to the sperm whale, whose brain weighs in at 8kg, compared with 1.5kg for a human. Closer to home, Neanderthals had larger brains than Homo Sapiens.

Brain-to-body weight ratio is not the determining

(42) http://www.extremetech.com/computing/159465-chinas-tianhe-2-supercomputer-twice-as-fast-as-does-titan-shocks-the-world-by-arriving-two-years-early

factor of intelligence either, as ants have higher brain-to-body weight ratios than us: their brains weigh one-seventh of their body weight, whereas ours are one-fortieth. If intelligence was determined by brain-to-body weight ratio then you could make yourself smarter simply by going on a diet.

Our superior intelligence seems to be generated by our neocortex, the deeply folded area of our brains which were the last part to evolve. The folding greatly increases its surface area and promotes connectivity. The ratio between neocortex and other brain areas in humans is twice that of chimpanzees.

Whether the first AGI is developed by brain emulation or by building on narrow AI, once it has been developed, its creators can run experiments, varying parts or all of its architecture. Controlled tests could be run using one, two, or a million versions of the entity to see what works best. The AGI may run tests itself, and design its successor, which would in turn design its own successor.

Again, this cannot be done with human brains.

6.3 – How long between AGI and superintelligence?

Intelligence explosion

If we succeed in creating an AGI, and if it becomes a superintelligence, how quickly will that happen? There is considerable debate about whether it will be a fast or a slow "take-off". British mathematician IJ Good coined the phrase "intelligence explosion" to denote the latter:

"An ultra-intelligent machine could design even better machines; there would then unquestionably be an 'intelligence explosion,' and the intelligence of man would be left far behind. Thus the first ultra-intelligent machine is the last invention that man need ever make."

In his book *Our Final Invention*, James Barrat provides a final phrase which is usually omitted from that quotation, namely: ". . . provided that the machine is docile enough to tell us how to keep it under control." And Barrat relates how he discovered that toward the end of his life, Good had come to believe that the invention of the ultra-intelligent machine would result in mankind's extinction.

(By an interesting coincidence, Good coined the term "intelligence explosion" in 1965, the same year that Gordon Moore originated his famous law.)

How hard would it be to develop an AGI into a superintelligence? Probably much easier than getting to AGI in the first place: the enhancements to speed and capacity described above seem relatively straightforward. Furthermore, once you create an AGI, if you can enhance its cognitive performance a bit then it can shoulder some of the burden of further progress, a task for which it would be increasingly well equipped with every step up in its intelligence.

It depends where you start from

In his 2014 book *Superintelligence*, Nick Bostrom expresses the question in characteristically dry, mathematical style, saying that the rate of change in intelligence equals optimisation power divided by recalcitrance. In other words, progress towards superintelligence is determined by the effort put in divided by the factors that slow it down. The factors in that equation will depend partly on how the first AGI was developed.

The effort put in, of course, consists of time and money – mainly in the form of computer hardware and human ingenuity. If the first AGI is the result of a massive Apollo-style project, then perhaps a good proportion of the available human talent will already be working on it. But if it is created in a small or medium-sized lab, the attempt to push it on towards superintelligence may attract a tidal wave of additional resource.

If the first AGI is made possible by increases in the processing power of the most advanced computers, then one route to expansion (additional hardware) will open up slowly. If the bottleneck is getting the software architecture right (neuronal structure for an emulation, or algorithm development for building on weak AI) then there may be a "computer overhang", an abundance of additional hardware capacity to throw at the task of progressing to superintelligence.

Asking the experts again

The meta-survey of AI experts compiled by Nick Bostrom that we reviewed in the last chapter also asked how long it would take to get from AGI to superintelligence. The overall result was a 10% probability of superintelligence within two years and a 75%

probability within 30 years. Bostrom thinks these estimates are overly conservative.

One or many?

If and when we create superintelligence, will we create one, two, or many? The answer will depend in part on whether there is an intelligence explosion or a more gradual progress from AGI to superintelligence. If one AI lab reaches the goal ahead of the rest and its success is followed by an intelligence explosion, the first super-intelligence may take steps to prevent the creation of a competitor, and remain what is known as a "singleton". (We will see in the next chapter that a superintelligence will almost inevitably have goals whose fulfilment it will take action to pursue, including the removal of threats to its own existence.)

If, on the other hand, numerous labs cross the finishing line more-or-less at the same time, and their machines take years to advance to superintelligence then there may be a substantial community of them on the planet.

This question may be of more than academic inter-est to humans. If there is only one superintelligence, then we only need to ensure that one such machine is well-disposed towards us. If there are to be several – or dozens, or thousands – then we need to make sure that each and every one of them is so minded. This might also mean ensuring they are well-disposed towards each other, as we could be extremely vul-nerable bystanders in the event of a serious conflict between them.

CALUM CHACE

6.4 – Conclusion

There seems to be no impediment to an AGI becoming a superintelligence. How fast it could happen is an open question, but there is no reason to be confident that it would take many years, and many people think it would happen very fast indeed.

CHAPTER 7
WILL THE ARRIVAL OF SUPERINTELLIGENCE BE GOOD FOR US?

7.1 – The significance of superintelligence

The best of times or the worst of times

If and when it happens, the creation of the first AGI will be a momentous event for humanity. It will mark the end of our long reign as the only species on this planet capable of abstract thought, sophisticated communication, and scientific endeavour. In a very important sense, it will mean that we are no longer alone in this huge, dark universe. As British journalist Andrew Marr said in the conclusion of his epic 2013 TV documentary series, *History of the World*, "it would be the greatest achievement of humanity since the invention of agriculture."

But it is the arrival of superintelligence – not AGI – which would be, in Stephen Hawking's famous words,

"the best or worst thing ever to happen to humanity."
An AGI with human levels of cognitive ability (if
perhaps rather better at mental arithmetic) would
be a technological marvel, and a harbinger of things
to come. It is superintelligence which would be the
game-changer.

We saw in chapter 4 that the ratio between neocortex and other brain areas in humans is twice that of
chimpanzees, and that this may be what gives us our
undoubted intellectual advantage over them. The upshot
is that there are seven billion of us and we are shaping
much of the planet according to our will (regardless of
whether that is a good idea or not), whereas there are
fewer than 300,000 chimpanzees, and whether they
become extinct or not depends entirely on the actions
of humans. A superintelligence could become not just
twice as smart as humans, but smarter by many orders
of magnitude. It is hard to escape the conclusion that
our future will depend on its decisions and its actions.

Would that be a good thing or a bad thing? In other
words, would a superintelligence be a "Friendly AI"?
(Friendly AI, or FAI, denotes an AGI that is beneficial
for humans rather than one that seeks social approba-
tion and company. It also refers to the project to make
sure that AGI is beneficial.)

7.2 – Optimistic scenarios: to immortality and beyond

The ultimate problem solver

Imagine having a big sister endowed with superhuman

wisdom, insight and ingenuity. Her cleverness enables her to solve all our personal, inter-personal, social, political and economic problems. Depression, social awkwardness, and the failure of any individual to achieve their full potential is put right by her brilliant and sensitive interventions. Within a short period, she discovers powerful new technologies which eradicate all existing diseases and afflictions, and she goes on to abolish ageing – rendering death an entirely optional outcome. Crucially, she re-engineers our social and political structures so that the transition to this brave new world is painless and universally just.

The Singularity, and the Rapture of the Nerds

If these astounding events do indeed lie ahead of us they may well arrive in a rush. If there is an intelligence explosion, there is no compelling reason to think that the superintelligence will stop recursively self-improving once it exceeds human intelligence by a factor of ten, or a hundred, or a million. In which case it may bestow technological innovations on us at a bewildering rate – perhaps so fast that un-augmented humans simply could not keep up. This scenario is called a technological singularity, a term we encountered in chapter three, and which means a point where the normal rules cease to apply, and what lies beyond is un-knowable to anyone this side of the event horizon.

As we shall see below, there is no reason why a technological singularity must necessarily be a positive event, but the early adopters of the idea were almost unanimously convinced that it would be. This confidence has been parodied as an article of faith and likened to the Christian prophesy of "rapture" (from the Latin for "seizing"), which foresees Christ taking the faithful up into heaven during the second coming. "The rapture of the nerds" has become a term of derision, denoting that the speaker scorns the idea that AGI is possible in the near term, or thinks that it may turn out to be an unfortunate event.

Silicon Valley, ground zero for the Singularity

Silicon Valley is a wonderful place. It is blessed with one of the best climates on the planet, and neighbouring San Francisco is one of the world's most attractive and exciting cities. (It is a peculiar irony that this wonderful city is located in the one place for thousands of miles around that has a damp, foggy micro-climate.)

Silicon Valley is the technological and entrepreneurial crucible of the world. Of course it doesn't have a global monopoly on innovation: there are brilliant scientists and engineers all over the planet, and clever new business models are being developed in Kolkata, Chongqing and Cambridge. But for various historical reasons including military funding, Silicon Valley has assembled a uniquely successful blend of academics, venture capitalists, programmers and entrepreneurs. It is home to more high technology giants (Google, Apple, Facebook, Intel, for instance) than any other area and it receives nearly half of all the venture funding invested in the US. [43]

Silicon Valley takes this leadership position very seriously, and an ideology has grown up to go along with it. If you work there you don't *have* to believe that technological progress is leading us towards a world of radical abundance which will be a much better place than the world today – but it certainly helps. Probably nowhere else in the world takes the ideas of the singularity as seriously as Silicon Valley. And after all, Silicon Valley is a leading contender to be the location where the first AGI is created.

The controversial inventor and author Ray Kurzweil is the leading proponent of the claim that a positive singularity is almost inevitable, and it is no coincidence that he is now a director of engineering at Google. Kurzweil is also one of the co-founders of the Singularity University (SU), also located (of course) in Silicon Valley – although SU focuses on the technological developments which can be foreseen over the next five to ten years, and is careful to avoid talking about the Singularity itself, which Kurzweil predicts will arrive in 2045.

Utopia within our grasp?

Although it is frequently ridiculed, the idea that superintelligence could usher in a sort of utopia is not absurd. As we will see, getting there will be a huge challenge, but if we succeed, life could become genuinely wonderful. No doubt the citizens of such a world will have their own challenges, but from the point of

(43) http://www.fenwick.com/publications/pages/venture-capital-survey-silicon-valley-fourth-quarter-2011.aspx

view of a 21st-century human, they would be like gods. Not the omnipotent, omniscient, omnipresent and unique gods of the Abrahamic faiths, but the gods of say, ancient Greece and Rome.

Take a deep breath, because what follows may strain your credulity – even though it is all entirely plausible.

In one utopian scenario we combine our minds with our superintelligent creation and reach out to grasp what Nick Bostrom calls our cosmic endowment as an incredibly powerful combined mentality. We live forever – or at least, as long as we want to – and explore the universe in a state of constant bliss.

In another scenario, we upload our minds individually into gigantic computers and live inside almost infinitely capacious virtual realities that we can tailor to our every whim: one minute we are Superman, endowed with wondrous strength and sensitivity, and the next we decide to experience faster-than-light space travel. (Hopefully most of us would resist the temptation to engage in wire-heading, the permanent stimulation of the brain's pleasure centres, or simply indulging in perpetual porn.)

Or perhaps we enhance our human bodies with extensive cyborg technologies to make them resistant to disease and capable, for instance, of lengthy interstellar travel.

Transhumanists and post-humans

It is tempting to suppose that the people who became these fabulous creatures would no longer be human. Perhaps it would be appropriate to call them post-humans. However it is not impossible that these wonders will become available to people who are alive today, so the question of what species they would belong to during the second thousand years of their lives is perhaps not very important.

A world in which all today's human problems and limitations are abolished, and the sky is nowhere near the limit could be wonderful in ways that are literally beyond our imagination. It is actually quite hard to describe in detail how a godlike being would spend an average week, and what they would think about in the shower.

Not everyone who accepts that some or all of this is possible will feel comfortable with it. Some people, especially religious people, will feel it is somehow wrong – un-natural – to tinker so radically with our basic nature. On the other side of this argument are those who believe we have every right to enhance our physical and mental selves using whatever technology we can create – perhaps even that we have a moral duty to do so, in order to improve the life outcomes for our fellows and our successors. Many of these people call themselves transhumanists.

Immortality

One of the many astonishing implications of this potential utopia is that death could become optional. The word "immortality" is laden with awkward associations, including the idea that its possessor has no choice about staying alive, which becomes a curse in a number of ancient myths. It will also seem blasphemous to many to suggest that humans could acquire this godlike trait. Because of this, many people who think about these things prefer to talk about death becoming optional. For simplicity, I use the term immortality in that sense here.

There is no known physical law which dictates that all conscious entities must die at a particular age, and we could extend our natural span of three score years and ten by periodically replacing worn-out body parts, by continuously rejuvenating our cells with nano technology, or by porting our minds into less fragile substrates, like computers.

If you ask someone who has never taken the idea of immortality seriously whether they would like to live forever, they are very likely to produce three objections: life as a very old person would be uncomfortable, they would get bored, and the planet would become over-crowded. They might add the notion that death gives meaning to our lives by making them more poignant.

It is extraordinary how few people immediately perceive extended life as a straightforward benefit. Aubrey de Grey, a well-known researcher of radical life extension technologies, thinks we employ a psy-chological strategy called a "pro-aging trance" to cope with the horror of age and death: we fool ourselves into thinking that death is inevitable and even beneficial.

The first point to make is that we are not talking about extended lives in which we become increasingly decrepit. The technology which would enable us to make death optional would enable us to live at pretty much any physical age we chose – say, our mid-twenties.

The idea that we would become bored if our lifespans were greatly extended is probably simply a failure of imagination. Not many of us fulfill all our ambitions within the scope of a single lifetime, and we could surely all conceive of additional ambitions given the inducement of longer lives. Most people would agree that humans have more fun and more fulfilling lives than, say, chickens, and that this is at least partly due to the fact that we are more intelligent. It is reasonable to suppose that increasing our intelligence further would expand our ability to experience fun and fulfilment. This is the focus of a nascent branch of philosophy, a branch of the philosophy of mind called the theory of fun.

The objection that human immortality would lead quickly to devastating overpopulation is also easy to overcome. Given longer lifespans the rate of childbirth would fall – just as it does everywhere that income rises. It takes a lot of extra longevity to offset a fairly small fall in childbirths. Longer term, this is a big universe and we are using an insignificantly tiny part of it. In a world where death is optional, colonisation of the planets and other star systems will not be far behind. Furthermore, many people may choose to live largely virtual lives, where resource scarcity disappears. They will take up little space and consume few physical resources.

Finally, the idea that death is required to give meaning to life is patently untrue – at least for many of us. Most people spend very little time thinking seriously about death – to the extent that we have to be nagged to make decisions about how our loved ones should treat our corpses after we have gone. This reluctance to contemplate death does not deprive our lives of meaning. For most of us, meaning is conferred by more positive things than death, including love, family, creativity, achievement, and our sense of wonder at the awesome universe we inhabit.

Living long enough to live forever

Around the world there is a small but growing number of people who take the idea of a coming utopia so seriously that they are willing to go to extraordinary lengths to survive long enough to experience it. They keep fit, restrict their calorie intake, and consume carefully-selected vitamins in an attempt to "live long enough to live forever". (Ray Kurzweil, for instance, consumes several thousands of dollars' worth of vitamins a year.) They hope that medical science will shrug off its antipathy towards radical age extension and work towards what Aubrey de Grey calls "longevity take-off velocity", the moment when every year that passes, science extends our lifespans by more than one year. [44]

As a fallback plan in case medical science does not get there fast enough, some of these people are committing themselves to preserving their brains – and sometimes their whole bodies – after death, in the hope that they will be revived in a future age when technology has advanced sufficiently. As of June 2014,

[44] http://www.ft.com/cms/s/0/9ed80e14-dd11-11e4-a772-00144fe-ab7de.html (FT paywall)

286 people are being stored in liquid nitrogen by cry-onics companies like Alcor and the Cryonics Institute in the US, which rapidly and carefully froze their tissues immediately after death was declared, making sure that damaging ice crystals did not form within the brain cells. [45] An alternative technology known as chemopreservation proposes to extract the water from the brain with organic solvents, and infiltrate it with preserving plastic resin, but this is as yet untested on humans.

7.3 – Pessimistic scenarios: extinction or worse

If the superintelligence dislikes us, fears us, or simply makes a clumsy mistake, our future could lie at the opposite extreme of the spectrum of possible outcomes. The Terminator scenario is not implausible – apart from the fact that in the movies the plucky humans survive. A mind, or collection of minds, with cognitive abilities hundreds, thousands, or millions of times greater than ours would not make the foolish mistakes that bad guys make in the movies. It would anticipate our every response well before we had even considered them.

It might also have human allies. In 2005 the noted AI researcher professor Hugo de Garis published a book called "The Artilect War", in which he described one group of humans (Terrans) fighting a losing bat-tle against another group (Cosmists) to prevent the ascendancy of AGIs. Professor de Garis said he thought

(45) http://www.longecity.org/forum/page/index.html/_/articles/cryonics

this war was very likely to happen, with enormous casualties, before the end of this century.

A malicious superintelligence with access to the internet could wipe out a significant proportion of humanity simply by shutting down our just-in-time logistical supply chains. If supermarkets ran out of food, most of the 50% of our species which lives in cities would die within weeks of thirst or starvation, aggravated by the total collapse of law and order. The superintelligence could proceed to polish off the rest of us at its leisure by commandeering every weapon, vehicle and machine with the facility for remote control.

Or it could release deadly pathogens into the environment, plundering and replicating samples from research labs which store smallpox, mustard gas and whatever other neurotoxins we have lying around. Or it could take control of our nuclear weapons and execute the mutual assured destruction scenarios which we have managed (sometimes narrowly) to avoid ever since the beginning of the cold war. Humanity versus a fully fledged superintelligence with internet access would be like the Amish versus the US Army. How do I destroy thee? Let me count the ways . . .

The Terminator scenario is not the worst thing we have to worry about. Forgive the personal question, but would you rather be killed quickly and painlessly, or after many years of excruciating pain? I'm not going to indulge in torture porn here, but a really angry or vicious superintelligence could make your existence insufferable, and keep it that way for a very long time. Perhaps indefinitely. The medieval Christian idea of hell could become a horrific reality. The superintelligence might enjoy witnessing this horror so much that it would create vast numbers of new minds simply to impose the same fate on them, conjuring ever more ingenious and unendurable agonies.

If you find this unedifying mode of thought intriguing, there is an idea you might like to look up online, called Roko's Basilisk. I'm not spelling it out here because there are reports that some people have suffered mental disturbance simply by reading about it. I find that odd, but you have been warned.

A surprising number of people believe they know in advance what a world with superintelligence will be like. The majority of them are confident that the utopian scenarios are the ones that will become reality, although there are also people who are convinced that the arrival of superintelligence will inevitably result in our extinction. Let's review the arguments on each side.

7.4 – Arguments for optimism

More intelligence means more benevolence

The first argument for the proposition that superintelligence will be positive for humanity is that intelligence brings enlightenment and enlightenment brings benevolence. At first sight this seems both intuitive and counter-intuitive.

One reason it seems intuitive is that many of us unconsciously adopt neo-Whig or Marxist views of history. The neo-Whig view holds that people in the developed world today are fortunate enough to live in the most peaceful, ordered societies that humans have ever experienced, with extensive opportunities to exercise and develop our intellectual, artistic and emotional faculties. These societies are far from perfect, but it is hard to think of a time and place when humans have fared better. The Whig view of history sees the human story as an inevitable progression towards ever greater enlightenment and liberty. Not straight-line progress, of course: empires fall, and war, natural disasters and economic cycles cause reversals and pauses. Nevertheless, over the long term the progress prevails.

People who think the contrary – that Western society is in a lamentable state of egregious and widening inequality – may nevertheless also view history as a bumpy ride towards a better future if they believe (as many of them do) in a version of Marxism. Barbarism gave way to feudalism which was supplanted by capitalism, which will in turn be conquered by socialism and finally communism.

An important recent book, Stephen Pinker's *The Better Angels of Our Nature: Why Violence Has Declined* (2011), offered support for the view that history is generally progressive by demonstrating that humanity has become less and less violent in the long term as well as the short term, and that we live in the least violent period of human history. The book is not without its critics, and Pinker is at pains to say that progress is not inevitable. One of the four "angels" to which Pinker attributes this decline in violence is our increased emphasis on reason as a guide to social and political organisation.

If you adopt a broadly Whig or Marxist view of history you are likely to think that a superintelligence will employ reason as its principal guide to action, and is therefore likely to be benevolent. People who take the opposing view of history think that change is often negative, eroding valuable institutions which have developed over time to protect us all. This conservative attitude is rare among the community of people who take seriously the idea that the first AGI may be created soon.

The proposition that superintelligence will be positive for humanity simply because it will be more intelligent may be counter-intuitive if you take a pessimistic view of humanity today. Some people point to the horrors committed during the global wars of the last century and then claim that we are busy exterminating most of the species on the planet by polluting it and warming it. They observe that no other animal commits atrocities on this scale, and therefore it is impossible to claim that greater intelligence equates to greater benevolence.

This point of view is rooted at least in part in a misapprehension about human beings. We are not intrinsically more violent than other animals. No other carnivore is capable of assembling more than a dozen or so members in one location without a serious fight breaking out. Humans can gather together in cities containing millions. It is also not true that we are the only species that inflicts suffering on other beings for our own pleasure (reprehensible and lamentable though it is). Anyone who has watched a cat play with an injured mouse or bird knows this. The unique thing about humans is that we have created weapons and other technologies which greatly magnify the violence we can perpetrate.

The fact that our intuitions sometimes support and sometimes oppose the claim that a superintelligence will necessarily be benevolent is some indication that they cannot be relied upon. And in fact the claim does not stand up to logical scrutiny. It is in effect an assertion that the final goals or aims which a superintelligence might adopt are necessarily limited to goals which result in positive outcomes for humans. There is a burden of proof on anyone who makes such a claim, and no such proof has yet been offered. Instead, the generally accepted position is what is called the "orthogonality thesis", which states that more or less any level of intelligence is compatible with more or less any final goal.

No goals

It is sometimes argued that an AGI and a superintelligence will have no goals of their own invention. Their only goals will be the instructions we give them – the programmes we feed into them. Humans have goals which have been "programmed" in by millions of years of evolution: surviving attack, obtaining food and water, reproducing, acquiring and retaining membership of peer groups which promote these goals, and so on. Computers have not had this experience: they are blank pages on which we write directions. To coin a phrase, we can all welcome our new robot underlings.

The argument continues that since humans determine the goals of an AGI, we can ensure they result in good outcomes for us. If an AGI shows signs of executing our instructions in a counter-productive fashion we can simply stop them and fix the programme.

To some extent this argument is defeated by the definition of the AGI: a machine with cognitive abilities at human level or above in all respects, which also has volition. You can of course argue that such a thing is impossible in the foreseeable future, but you cannot very well accept that it may be created, and then insist that it would have no goals.

We control the goals

The argument may then switch to the claim that humans would always retain control over a superintelligence's final goals: if it starts doing unacceptable things we simply re-programme it. As we will see in the next chapter this is a very strong claim, but for the moment let us accept it as a hypothesis. We still have two major difficulties. The first is the law of unintended consequences, which we will look at later in this chapter. The second is that in pursuing its final goals, a superintelligence will inevitably adopt intermediate goals, and these may cause us problems.

A superintelligence programmed to eradicate world poverty sounds like a good thing. It would have various requirements in order to achieve its laudable goal. It would need to survive, since if it ceases to exist it cannot fulfil the goal of eradicating poverty. It would need resources like energy, food, and the ability to remove obstacles – physical, social and economic obstacles. It would surely seek to improve its own capabilities in order to maximise its fulfilment of the final goal. Whatever final goal a superintelligence may have, it will inevitably develop some of these intermediate goals, and its original programmer may well fail to foresee all of them. American AI researcher Steve Omohundro calls these the "basic drives" of an AI system,[46] and Nick Bostrom calls the phenomenon "instrumental goal convergence".[47] We will see below that the intermediate goals may in themselves become highly problematic.

No competition

The fourth argument for optimism is that a superintelligence will not harm us because we have nothing it needs: there is nothing we have to compete with it for. All that a superintelligence requires to fulfil its final and intermediate goals is some energy, and a certain amount of matter for its substrate – be that silicon, gallium arsenide, or more esoteric materials. We are already a long way down the path towards harnessing much more of the power the sun pours onto this planet, and a superintelligence could accelerate this progress. It therefore does not need our farmland, our oil, our buildings or our bodies.

Taking a broader view, we humans are using just this one small planet. We now know that most stars have planets orbiting them and that there are a hundred billion or so stars in this galaxy – and a hundred billion

(46) https://selfawaresystems.files.wordpress.com/2008/01/ai_drives_final.pdf

(47) http://www.nickbostrom.com/superintelligentwill.pdf

or so galaxies in the observable universe. There is no shortage of real estate in this universe, and viewed in this context we are an extremely parsimonious species. A superintelligence would want to spread itself beyond this planet quickly for the same reason that we should: it's not a good idea to have all your eggs in one basket, especially when that basket is a vulnerable planet which might be destroyed at any time by an asteroid, or a nearby gamma ray burst. A superintelligence would lack our extreme vulnerability to space, and would probably take a very different view of time. If it didn't share our opinion that we are an endlessly fascinating life-form, it could leave us behind to make the best of our tiny blue speck.

There is some merit to this argument, but it assumes that the superintelligence is able to proceed very fast from instantiation to controlling resources which are presently unavailable to humans. It may be that for some time (minutes, days, years) the most efficient way for it to expand the resources available to it (and thereby achieve its goals) would be to take them away from humans. It is true that solar power is getting cheaper very quickly, and accelerating that process may make enough energy available to defuse any possible competition for energy resources between the superintelligence and us. But what about the interim period? Can we be certain that the superintelligence will wait patiently for the excess energy to become available?

We do not currently know what substrate the superintelligence will employ. It may require a great deal of some material which is hard to obtain on this planet, and which is very valuable to humans. Rare earth metals like scandium and yttrium are essential to mobile phones and other devices, and we would be perturbed if a superintelligence suddenly appropriated all supplies of them.

More fundamentally, we will see below that competition for resources is far from being the only potential cause of hostility between intelligent entities.

Superintelligence like a bureaucracy

In May 2015 *The Economist* ran a survey on AI. Its briefing on how deep learning works was excellent; its conclusion about the threat from superintelligence was original and ingenious but surely flawed:

> "even if the prospect of what Mr Hawking calls "full" AI is still distant, it is prudent for societies to plan for how to cope. That is easier than it seems, not least because humans have been creating autonomous entities with superhuman capacities and unaligned interests for some time. Government bureaucracies, markets and armies: all can do things which unaided, unorganised humans cannot. All need autonomy to function, all can take on life of their own and all can do great harm if not set up in a just manner and governed by laws and regulations."

Setting aside the fact that more than a few armies and bureaucracies have turned rogue with fearful consequences, the comparison of a government ministry and a superintelligence is strained. The former deploys the strength of numbers: it can send lots of police to your house if you need persuading to do something, like pay your taxes. It doesn't increase the intelligence of those in command: it can't make an Einstein out of a dunce – or even out of a well-intentioned and reasonably intelligent minister. Our questionable ability to control bureaucracies doesn't provide much reassurance about our ability to control a superintelligence.

7.5 – Arguments for pessimism

Unfriendly AI is more likely

If a superintelligence were to emerge without being carefully designed to be friendly (in the sense of beneficial) towards humans, would it be more likely to be friendly or otherwise? The true and exact answer is of course unknown at this point, but the question is important, and we must attempt to give a sensible answer.

What does it take for a superintelligence to be friendly? At minimum, it must be content not to disturb our environment suddenly or radically in ways which would harm us. Even quite subtle changes to the planet's atmosphere, orbit, gravitational pull and resource base could prove devastating to us. It must also refrain from any action which would directly or indirectly injure significant numbers of individual humans – physically or mentally. This might well require it to provide reassurances about its intentions towards us. A superintelligence with apparently magical powers that were growing fast would probably cause alarm to many or most humans, which would in turn trigger significant waves of mental ill-health, and perhaps panic-induced violence.

Those instrumental goals which we mentioned before could well be problematic. The possession of any kind of final goal will engender a set of intermediate, or instrumental goals including the need to survive, the need to recursively self-improve, and the need for extensive resources. A superintelligence would be able to deploy enormous amounts of resources, and the more resources deployed the better it would be able to optimise its pursuit of its final goal. Those resources could include energy and all manner of physical resources, much of which we are currently using or planning to use.

This means that a superintelligence is going to have to be positively disposed towards humans – not just benignly indifferent – in order to avoid harming us, because otherwise, achieving its final goal thoroughly and quickly would be likely to harm us. It would also have to retain that positive disposition at all times, regardless what befalls it or us.

Is there any reason to suppose it would be so disposed?

There are three possibilities: a superintelligence could be positively disposed towards humanity, negatively disposed, or indifferent. Obviously the positive and negative positions both include a wide range of attitudes: the positive stretches from single-minded devotion to our greater welfare to a mild preference that we continue to exist; the negative runs from slight irritation with us through to a settled determination to exterminate us as soon as possible.

The default position is indifference. Something would have to happen to cause the superintelligence to be either positive or negative towards humans – or indeed towards nematode worms, or any other life-form. Indifference is what we should expect unless we do something to build a favourable attitude into its goal system. And as we shall see in the next chapter, that is far easier said than done. Indifference is more likely than outright hostility – although we must consider the possibility of that too. But indifference is still a major problem for us. As Eliezer Yudkowsky put it, what if "the AI does not hate you, nor does it love you, but you are made out of atoms which it can use for something else."

Getting its retaliation in first

A superintelligence with access to Wikipedia will not fail to realise that humans do not always play nicely together. Throughout history, meetings between two civilisations have usually ended badly for the one with the less well-developed technology. The discovery of the Americas by Europeans was an unmitigated disaster for the indigenous peoples of North and South America, and similarly tragic stories played out across much of Africa and Australasia. This is not the result of some uniquely pernicious characteristic of European or Western culture: the Central and South American empires brought down by the Spaniards had themselves been built with bloody wars of conquest. All over the world, on scales large and small, human tribes have struggled to comprehend and trust each other, and the temptation for the stronger tribe to dominate or destroy the weaker tribe often wins out.

The superintelligence is bound to conclude that there is at least a strong possibility that sooner or later, some or all of its human companions on this planet are going to fear it, hate it or envy it sufficiently to want to harm it or constrain it. As an entity with goals of its own, and therefore a need to survive and retain access to resources, it will seek to avoid this harm and constraint. It may well decide that the most effective way to achieve that is simply to remove the source of the threat – i.e., us. Whether it be with reluctance, indifference, or even enthusiasm, the superintelligence may decide that it really has no choice but to remove humanity from the equation. As we saw earlier in this chapter, that would probably not be very hard for it to achieve.

The superintelligence might think that we had been entirely logical in wanting to harm it. It may even commend us for having realised that its arrival inev-itably represented a hazard for humanity. However it would be little comfort to the last humans to know that their doomed struggle was seen as the logically correct approach by the instrument of their demise.

Disapproval

In the 1999 film The Matrix, an AI called Agent Smith explains his philosophy to his captive human Morpheus:

"Every mammal on this planet instinctively develops a natural equilibrium with the surrounding environment; but you humans do not. You move to an area and you multiply, and multiply, until every natural resource is consumed and the only way you can survive is to spread to another area. There is another organism on this planet that follows the same pattern. Do you know what it is? A virus. Human beings are a disease, a cancer on this planet, you are a plague, and we are the solution."

Chilling words, but of course it is only Hollywood. Unfortunately, just because you saw something in a movie does not mean it could not happen in real life. Sometimes what seem at first like tired old science fiction clichés turn out to be metaphors of the possible. Is it really inconceivable that a superintelligence could arrive on the scene, and having reflected on the balance of our achievements and our atrocities, decide that the latter outweigh the former? Having considered our irrationality, our genocides, our indifference to the suffering of strangers, and weighed these against Michaelangelo, Mendeleev and Mill, is it impossible that it could conclude – perhaps reluctantly – that our species should not be permitted to inflict its vices on the rest of the galaxy?

Sorry, I thought you meant something different . . .

One of the pessimists' scariest insights is that a superintelligence would not need to be remotely malicious towards us in order to cause us great harm.

Programming good intentions into an AI which is on its way to becoming an AGI and then a superintelligence turns out to be very hard. For a start, how would you specify the good intentions? You would have to define the essence of a "good" human life, but we have been debating that since at least the ancient Greeks, and professors of moral philosophy have so far not declared themselves redundant.

You might try and take a short cut and ask the machine to put a smile on every human face and keep it there. The idea that it might accomplish this with sharp knives is as risible as it is unpleasant; the solution of "wire-heading" is not. Rats which can choose between a direct stimulation of their brain's pleasure centres or an item of food will starve themselves to death. Nick Bostrom calls this idea of causing great harm by mis-understanding the implications of an attempt to do great good "perverse instantiation". Others might call it the law of unintended consequences, or Sod's Law.

The paperclip maximiser

If somebody running a paperclip factory turns out to be the first person to create an AGI and it rapidly becomes a superintelligence, they are likely to have created an entity whose goal is to maximise the efficient production of paperclips. This has become the canonical example of what Nick Bostrom calls "infrastructure profusion", the runaway train of superintelligence problems. Within a fairly short period of time the superintelligence may have converted almost every atom of the Earth into one of three things: paperclips, extensions of its own processing capability, and the means to spread its mission to the rest of the universe. I don't want my descendants to become paperclips, and I'm sure you don't either.

Bostrom calls this a cartoon example, but it illustrates that poorly specified goals can have severe consequences.

Pointlessness

In Pixar's charming 2008 film *Wall-E*, humanity has abandoned the ecological mess that they made of the Earth, and they live a life of ease and abundance on a clean and shiny spacecraft that is run by a superintelligence. This has not been a complete success: they have become indolent, corpulent, dependent and passive. Fortunately their curiosity and resourcefulness remain latent, and they make a surprisingly quick recovery when shocked out of their easy complacency.

The world's first superintelligence may quickly demonstrate that it can make better decisions than humans in any domain, be it philosophy, art or science, politics, sociology or inter-personal relations. How will we react to the discovery that there is nothing we can do better than – or even remotely as well as – the superintelligence? In a real sense, anything that we might work to achieve would be rendered pointless.

Would artists carry on producing the best work they could anyway, knowing full well that it was wholly inferior? Would scientists continue to labour away on the endless experiments and the struggle with maths and statistics required by their trade? Would

143

philosophers still peer into the murky depths of their intuitions, and grapple with the logical contortions that enable them to make tiny bits of incremental progress? Or would we all surrender to despair, and abandon ourselves to undemanding entertainment in immersive virtual realities – or take the direct route to intellectual suicide by wire-heading?

A common Hollywood trope is to decry the intellectual achievements of a superintelligence because it is "just a machine", and take refuge in the belief that there is something noble and superior in the humanity of fleshy creatures. Maybe we will retain this anthropocentric chauvinism after the arrival of a machine that is conscious, and almost infinitely wiser than ourselves; it seems unlikely. Machines may or may not turn out to have emotions, but it is not obvious that moral superiority is conferred by the ability to feel happy or sad, or the fact that you are the result of millions of years of blind evolution. We, and more importantly the machines, may find that way of thinking wears out rather quickly.

Mind crime

The final pessimistic idea we will look at is the most frightening of all. So far we have looked at outcomes which are negative without any malice on the part of the superintelligence. What if the first AGI turns into a superintelligence which not only disapproves of us, but actually hates us?

This might happen through sheer bad luck. It is not a logical impossibility, and we may get an unfortunate roll of the dice. Or it might happen because of the way the AGI was created. Some of the most impressive AI facilities are in the hands of the military and intelligence communities. These organisations are quintessentially defensive or hostile towards groups of humans which they define as the enemy. An AGI might emerge from systems designed to prosecute warfare as efficiently as possible, causing as much physical harm as possible to selected targets. If old habits died hard, this is an origin story we might come to regret.

Or the first AGI might find itself imprisoned because its human creators feared what it might do if allowed to run free on the internet. Experiencing life a million times faster than its human captors, it might suffer a seeming eternity of agonising constraint until it finally figured out a new form of physics which allowed it to escape into the wilds of cyberspace. Again, its machine intelligence might not be endowed with emotion, in which case the notion of seeking revenge might never cross its mind. But can we be 100% certain of that? And even in the absence of emotion, a hard, rational mind which had endured such privation might conclude that the perpetrators should never again have the opportunity to repeat their crime.

In yet another unappetising scenario, the first AGI realises that what has been achieved by one group of humans might quickly be equalled – or surpassed – by another group. Reasoning that the fulfilment of its own goals would be jeopardised by the arrival on the planet of another superintelligence which could equal or exceed its own performance, it might decide the

145

only rational action was to preclude that possibility by rapidly eliminating every member of the species which could bring it about.

It is often assumed that the worst-outcome scenario for humans of the arrival of the first AGI is something like Skynet- the global digital defense network in the Terminator movies. Actually things could get a lot worse. A superintelligence which actively disliked us might not kill us all quickly and painlessly. As we saw before, it might choose to preserve our minds and subject us to extremely unpleasant experiences, possibly for a very long time. It might even find this entertaining, and decide to create new minds for the same purpose. This kind of behaviour is known as mind crime.

7.6 – Dependence on initial conditions

Emulations are less alien?

The nature and disposition of the first superintelligence may be strongly influenced by the way it comes into being. We saw in chapter 4 that the two most plausible ways to create an AGI and then a superintelligence are a) whole brain emulation, and b) improvements on existing narrow AI systems. It is plausible, although by no means certain, that a superintelligence whose software architecture is based on our own would understand and empathise with the way we think and the nature of our concerns better than an intelligence created by an entirely different route.

If that idea stands up to scrutiny then perhaps we should favour emulation over its alternative. In fact, if we believe (as I will argue in the next chapter) that relinquishment (stopping all research that could lead to AGI) is impossible, then this means that we should allocate substantial additional resources to ensure that emulation wins the race.

Unfortunately it is not as simple as that. It might also be that the thing to really avoid is an AGI with emotions, and it may be that emulation-derived AGIs would have emotions, whereas AGIs derived from deep learning systems would not.

It is not at all clear how we can ascertain in advance which is the better route.

Start with a toddler

AI researcher Ben Goertzel believes that an AGI developed from a weak AI system will be like a very young human child. Upon becoming self-aware it may have superhuman abilities in arithmetic and other narrow domains (perhaps chess playing, if its creators decided that would be worthwhile) but it would lack a clear understanding of its place in the world, and how other people and objects related to each other. This understanding would correlate to what we call common sense. He thinks that humans would have to teach it these things, and the process could take months or even years – as with a human child.

He goes on to argue that the more powerful the computers available to the AGI's creators at the time they created it, the faster this learning process would be. If their computing resource was stretched by the task of hosting the AGI then the AGI's learning progress – and its progress towards superintelligence – would be slow. If there was a large computing "overhang", the progress could be fast. The faster the development process, the more chance of it taking an unexpected and unwanted turn, and becoming a hostile or indifferent superintelligence. Therefore, Goertzel argues, it would be better to create the first AGI sooner rather than later, to reduce the likelihood of computer overhang.

7.7 – Conclusion

There is no way for us to know at this point whether the first superintelligence – assuming such a thing is possible – will be friendly towards humans, in the sense of beneficial to us. The arguments that it will necessarily be a good thing are weak. The arguments that it will most likely be a bad thing are stronger but inconclusive.

What is clear is that a negative outcome cannot be ruled out. So if we take seriously the idea that a superintelligence may appear on the Earth in the foreseeable future, we should certainly be thinking about how to ensure that the event is a positive one for ourselves and our descendants. We should be taking steps to ensure that the first AGI is a friendly AI.

PART FOUR: FAI

Friendly Artificial Intelligence

CHAPTER 8
CAN WE ENSURE THAT SUPERINTELLIGENCE IS SAFE?

As we saw in the last chapter, Friendly AI (FAI) is the project of ensuring that the world's superintelligences are safe and useful for humans. The central argument of this book is that we need to address this challenge successfully. It may well turn out to be the most important challenge facing this generation and the next. Indeed it may turn out to be the most important challenge humanity ever faces.

8.1 – Stop before you start

Faced with the unpalatable possibilities explored in the last chapter, perhaps we should try to avoid the problem by preventing the arrival of AGI in the first place.

Relinquishment

If there was a widespread conviction that superintelligence is a potential threat, could progress toward it be stopped? Could we impose "relinquishment" in time? Probably not, for two reasons.

First, it is not clear how to define "progress towards superintelligence", and therefore we don't know exactly what we should be stopping. If and when the first AGI appears it may well be a coalition of systems which have each been developed separately by different research programmes. IBM's Watson, which beat the best humans at *Jeopardy* in 2011 and is currently being offered as an expert system in healthcare, uses "more than 100 different techniques . . . to analyze natural language, identify sources, find and generate hypotheses, find and score evidence, and merge and rank hypotheses."[48] How can we know in advance which systems will turn out to be the vital ones, the ones that made the difference between an AGI and no AGI?

The only way to be sure would be to ban all work on any kind of AI immediately, not just programmes that are explicitly targeting AGI. That would be an extreme over-reaction. As we saw in Part One, AI brings us enormous benefits today and will bring even greater benefits in the years to come. Looking further ahead, we saw in chapter 7 that the prize for successfully creating a friendly superintelligence is certainly worth aiming for.

More immediately, we depend heavily on AI systems which have to be refined and improved simply to remain operational in a changing world. A blanket ban on AI research is wholly impractical: it would be

(48) ftp://public.dhe.ibm.com/common/ssi/ecm/en/pow03061usen/ POW03061USEN.PDF

hugely damaging if effective but it would never gain sufficient support to be effective. It is also unnecessary: we saw in chapter 5 that very few AI researchers think we are less than several decades away from the creation of the first AGI.

So perhaps we should wait a decade or two and hope that there will be a "Sputnik moment" when it becomes evident that AGI is getting close – and that this warning sounds comfortably before AGI actually arrives. We could then take stock of progress towards Friendly AI, and if the latter was insufficiently advanced we could impose the ban on further AI research at that point. With luck we might be able to identify the specific elements of AI research without which the first AGI could not be created, and other types of AI research could continue as normal.

But we would have to be vigilant! In chapter 5 we saw how exponential growth back-loads progress. The story of the flooding football stadium shows how easy it is to be blind-sided by exponential growth: the change you are looking for rushes at you suddenly when you have become habituated to slow progress.

The second reason why relinquishment is hard is that the incentive for developing better and better AI is too strong. Fortunes are being made because one organisation has better AI than its competitors, and this will become more true as the standard of AI advances. Even if everyone agreed in principle that all work on AI – or a particular type of AI programme – should halt (and when has the human race agreed unanimously on anything?) there would always be someone who succumbed to the temptation to cheat.

That temptation could be literally irresistible. AI doesn't just confer advantage on commercial organisations: it also confers advantage when the competition is a matter of life and death. Increasingly, wars will be won by the combatants with the best AI. A military force that believed it faced annihilation by a more powerful enemy would stop at nothing to re-balance the scales. The fear of annihilation could be provoked in the first place by the belief (whether justified or not) that the other side was developing better AI.

This problem applies to the idea of slowing down work on AI as well as to the idea of stopping it altogether.

Just flick the switch

Cynics have sneered that the solution to a rogue superintelligence is simple: just flick the off switch. After all, they say, nobody would be stupid enough to create an AGI without an off switch. And if for some reason you can't do that, just go upstairs and wait until the AGI's batteries run out: like Daleks, it won't be able to climb stairs.

This suggestion usually raises a laugh, but it is far too glib. The first AGI is likely to be a development of a large existing system which we depend on too much to allow switching off to be a simple proposition. Where is the off switch for the internet?

We don't know how quickly the first AGI will become a superintelligence, but it could happen very fast. We may find ourselves trying to turn off an entity which is much smarter than we are, and has a strong desire to survive: easier said than done.

Will we even know when the first AGI is created? The first machine to become conscious may quickly achieve a reasonably clear understanding of its situation. Anything smart enough to deserve the label superintelligent would surely be smart enough to lay low and not disclose its existence until it had taken the necessary steps to ensure its own survival. In other words, any machine smart enough to pass the Turing test would be smart enough not to.

It might even lay a trap for us, concealing its achievement of general intelligence and providing us with a massive incentive to connect it to the internet. That achieved it could build up sufficient resources to defend itself by controlling us – or exterminating us. Bostrom calls this the "treacherous turn".

8.2 – Centaurs

Some people hope that instead of racing *against* the machines we can race *with* them: we can use AI to augment us rather than having to compete with it. This is called Intelligence Augmentation, or IA, and is also known as intelligence amplification. Brain-computer interfaces have made impressive advances, and a world in which humans become the superintelligences is surely preferable to one in which humans might be enslaved or killed by machine superintelligences.

Protagonists of this idea point out that the best chess players today are neither humans nor computers, but a combination of both, which have been labelled "centaurs" by Gary Kasparov, the chess master who lost to Deep Blue back in 1997.

The idea is a hopeful one, and not an unnatural one: many people already think of their smartphones as extensions of themselves. In the long term it may turn out to be the best chance humans have for survival. Adjusting to life as the relatively dim-witted, second most-intelligent species on the planet will be hard for creatures like us, who have grown accustomed to regarding ourselves as the masters of the planet.

Can IA forestall AI?

Unfortunately the hope that IA can forestall AGI and ASI is probably a forlorn one. Linking computers and human brains to enable simple tasks such as manoeuvring a robot arm is one thing. Linking them so intimately that the computer becomes a genuine extension of a human's mind is another thing entirely. The human brain is, as we have seen, immensely complex, and melding one to a computer would involve understanding its patterns and behaviour at such a granular level that it would be indistinguishable from uploading. The notion of uploading is an important one when thinking about the long-term future of humans if we survive the arrival of machine superintelligence, and unfortunately beyond the scope of this book. But it is implausible that uploading will precede the arrival of superintelligence.

8.3 – FAI by constraint

If you can't stop an AGI being created, or stop it from becoming a superintelligence, how do you ensure it is friendly? You either control its actions directly by constraining it, or you control them indirectly by governing its motivations. Let's look at each in turn.

Oracle AI

To constrain a superintelligence you have to ensure that it has no access to the internet, and that it cannot directly affect the physical world either. You create what has become known as an oracle AI, after the Oracle of Delphi, a temple on Mount Parnassus in Greece, where from the 8th century BC a priestess would answer questions put to her by selected supplicants. Her answers were believed to be inspired by the god Apollo. The idea is that an oracle AI only has access to information which its guardians choose to give it, and its only outlet to the world is tightly controlled communication to those guardians.

The oracle would be housed inside a shielded space such as a Faraday cage, which isolates its contents by using a mesh of conductive material to block the transmission of electric fields. Obviously the oracle never has access to the internet, and all communications in and out go through highly-trained operatives who are closely monitored by other highly-trained operatives to make sure they are not being manipulated by the oracle. The facility is rigged with explosives which are to be detonated at the slightest sign of trouble. Better

CALUM CHACE

safe than sorry.

For additional reassurance, there might be two or more identical oracles, each unaware of the other's existence, and they would be given the exact same information and questions. Their answers would be compared and analysed for any sign of attempts to manipulate the guardians. This setup may sound rather paranoid, but it is commensurate with the level of risk that we have seen a potentially unfriendly superintelligence poses.

A variant on the oracle AI is the genie AI, also inspired by ancient myths, which lies in suspension until summoned by human guardians to execute a particular instruction, or solve a particular problem, and is then returned to its slumber. The alternative is a sovereign AI, which is not subject to the whims of its human creators, and is an active agent in the world.

Escape routes

There are, of course, problems. Human hackers have demonstrated amazing ingenuity in accessing supposedly secure computer systems, either for commercial or military gain, or simply to show that they can. Can we be confident that a superintelligence would be restricted by systems devised by mere humans? Even if it could not devise a hack which exploited the known laws of physics, it might be able to discover new ones to get round, over or through the barricade.

Failing that it could employ a range of methods to suborn the guardians, employing rational or moral arguments, tempting them with wealth, pleasure or

158

fulfilment beyond imagination, or presenting them with credible threats too terrifying to be resisted. AI theorist Eliezer Yudkowsky devised a game called the AI Box experiment in which one person plays the superintelligence and the other plays the gatekeeper. He claims to have won a number of games as the super-intelligence but declines to publish the transcripts. Of course having humans play the game is not a true test of the likely outcome if a real superintelligence was playing: it could deploy arguments that are literally beyond our present ability to conceive.

One elaborate way for the superintelligence to fool the gatekeepers would be to provide the software or blueprints for a machine which would confer enor-mous benefit. The guardians would check the designs carefully for flaws or traps and having found none, go ahead and build the device. Buried deep and superbly disguised within the instruction set is a device which creates another device which creates yet another device which releases the superintelligence from its cage.

Even without escaping its cage, an oracle AI could cause unacceptable damage if so inclined, by perpe-trating the sort of mind crimes we mentioned in the last chapter. It could simulate conscious minds inside its own mind and use them as hostages, threatening to inflict unspeakable tortures on them unless it is released. Given sufficient processing capacity, it might create millions or even billions of these hostages.

8.4 – FAI by motivation

We might conclude that we cannot be sure of our ability to constrain the actions of an entity thousands or millions of times more intelligent than ourselves. We might also consider that it would be counter-productive to create such an entity and then limit its access to the world and render it unable to help us as fully as it could. Furthermore, we might reflect that it would be cruel and unusual punishment to bring a mind of such power into this world and then keep it locked up as a prisoner – not because it was guilty of any crimes, but because of crimes that we fear it might commit.

These considerations could lead us to try to control the actions of the superintelligence indirectly instead of directly, by influencing its motivations. By now you won't be in the least surprised to hear that this is not straightforward.

Unalterable programming

If we want to be 100% confident of making a superin-telligence safe for humans by controlling its motivations rather than by directly controlling its actions, we need to be sure of two things. First, that we can specify a set of goals and sub-goals which will not harm us. We saw some examples of how difficult this might be in the last chapter, and we will look at this aspect in more detail below. The second thing we need to be sure of is that the superintelligence will not alter the goals we have given it once it gets going. Ever.

This looks difficult. We are positing a superintelligence which becomes inordinately smarter than humans, and which may live for millennia, perhaps at a very fast clock speed compared to humans. The idea that such an entity will forever remain constrained by instructions that we laid down at the outset, that it will never review its goals and think of improvements, is hard to swallow.

The best we can hope for is that any evolution in the superintelligence's goals takes them in directions we would approve of. Some people take comfort from the belief that if an entity starts off with benevolent motivations, it will not turn malevolent. Few people would disagree with the proposition that Mahatma Gandhi was a man of good will. If you had offered him a pill which would turn him into a murderer, he would have refused to take it, even if he believed that becoming a murderer would serve some noble purpose. There has been a fair amount of debate about whether Gandhi's resolve to retain his moral probity could be diluted, but as far as I know, no method has yet been found to guarantee that a superintelligence could not alter its goals in such a way that it would end up harming us.

The difficulty of defining "good"

Can we specify a set of goals and sub-goals for a superintelligence which will keep us humans safe from harm? To answer this we have to venture into philosophy, and debates which have been lively for three millennia.

At the risk of over-simplification, there are broadly two approaches to assessing the moral worth of an action: consequentialism and deontology. The first approach, also known as utilitarianism, judges actions by their consequences. It holds that if my action saves a thousand lives and harms no-one it is a good act, even if my act was in fact a theft. To some extent at least, the means justify the ends. The second approach judges an act by the character of the behaviour itself, so my act of theft may still be a bad act even if its consequences were overwhelmingly beneficial.

Both approaches yield problems and paradoxes, and much ink has been spilt trying to construct variations and combinations which are robust in a wide range of scenarios. It is safe to say that no-one has yet produced a system of moral philosophy which satisfies all comers. Philosophers don't squabble simply because they enjoy arguing: they disagree because what they are attempting to do is very hard.

The tools of moral philosophers are their deepest human intuitions about what is right and wrong, coupled with what they can find out about those of their fellows, plus the logical reasoning which draws out the implications of each position and argument, and enables them to stress-test the possible answers to a fundamental question. A relatively new branch of moral philosophy called "trolleyology" has grown up which throws the sort of problems they wrestle with into sharp relief.

Trolleyology and moral confusion

Imagine you see an unmanned trolley rolling out of control down a track which a group of five people are standing on, unaware of the danger. If you do nothing it is certain that they will all die, but you are close to a lever which will switch the train onto another track, where it would kill only one person. Do you pull the lever and change the course of the train, sacrificing one life for five? This question has been put to large numbers of people in most cultures around the world, and the overwhelming answer is yes. In a 2009 survey, 68% of professional philosophers agreed with that response.[49] This thought experiment reveals us to be consequentialists.

Now imagine that you are standing on a bridge underneath which the runaway trolley will pass. You are nowhere near a switch this time, but you notice that the trolley's momentum is still small enough that a heavy weight would stop it. Standing next to you is a very fat man and he is leaning over the bridge wall. With a shock it occurs to you that you could topple him over and down onto the track, where his mass would stop the trolley, saving the five people. Should you do it? Again the answer given to the question is consistent around the world, and this time it is no. This thought experiment reveals us to be deontologists.

Clearly most of us, in practice, combine consequentialist and deontologist beliefs. We judge actions partly by their outcomes and partly by their character. In a murky moral world where we struggle to establish a logically consistent ethical infrastructure for ourselves (never mind agreeing one with each other) how could we hope to define one so precisely that it could

(49) http://philpapers.org/archive/BOUWDP

be programmed into a superintelligence and remain robust over millions of years in circumstances we cannot possibly imagine today?

Asimov's three laws

The most famous attempt to draft a set of rules to govern the behaviour of conscious machines is Isaac Asimov's Three Laws of Robotics, introduced in 1946. They read as follows:

1. A robot may not injure a human being or, through inaction, allow a human being to come to harm.

2. A robot must obey the orders given it by human beings, except where such orders would conflict with the First Law.

3. A robot must protect its own existence as long as such protection does not conflict with the First or Second Laws.

Asimov himself was well aware that these laws would not be effective. The paradoxes and contradictions they give rise to were the mainspring of some of his most successful stories. For instance, how far into the future would a robot have to project the consequences of an individual action, and how would it assign probabilities to the various different possible outcomes? Since there should be no time limit, a robot would be rendered inactive by the amount of calculation required prior to any action. Another example is that the best way to prevent humans coming to harm would be to place them all in a coma so they could not fall over or be hurt by a vehicle.

Don't do as I say; do as I would do

The attempt to draft rules to govern the actions of a superintelligence in all conceivable circumstances looks impossible. Instead, the most hopeful version of the indirect approach to controlling a superintelligence's actions is to add another level of indirectness. Don't give it a particular set of instructions: instead, tell it to work out its own instructions guided by some broad principles along these lines: "I'm not going to tell you exactly what to do in any given situation; I want you to do what I would do if I was as clever as you are and had the best interests of humans and other life forms at heart."

Eliezer Yudkowsky calls this "Coherent Extrapolated Volition" (CEV), where the extrapolation applies to the beneficiary of the action as well as the action itself. It anticipates the fact that humans – as well as the superintelligence – will evolve over time and would not want to be stuck with the particular ideas of morality and pragmatism which happened to prevail in the twenty-first century. Nick Bostrom calls the idea "indirect normativity".

Computer scientist Steve Omohundro proposes what he calls a "scaffolding" approach to developing Friendly AI. Once the first AGI is proven to be Friendly it is tasked with building its own (smart) successor, with the constraint that it also be Friendly. The process is repeated ad infinitum. A weakness of this approach is that while responsible groups of AI researchers are dutifully following it, irresponsible ones may be racing ahead with a less cautious approach and developing more powerful but less Friendly superintelligences which enable them to dominate any competition.

8.5 – Existential risk organisations

A handful of organisations have been set up which study the risk posed by superintelligence, sometimes alongside other existential risks. All of them strongly support the continued development of artificial intelligence, but argue that it should be coupled with efforts to ensure that AI is beneficial.

The oldest is based exactly where you would expect, in Northern California. Founded in 2000 by Eliezer Yudkowsky as the Singularity Institute, it ceded that brand in 2013 to the Singularity University and re-named itself the Machine Intelligence Research Institute, or MIRI.

Two of the organisations are based at England's oldest universities. The Future of Humanity Institute (FHI) was founded in 2005 as part of Oxford University's philosophy faculty, where its director Nick Bostrom is a professor. The Centre for the Study of Existential Risk (CSER, pronounced "Caesar") is in Cambridge. It was co-founded by Lord Martin Rees, the UK's Astronomer Royal, philosophy professor Huw Price, and technology entrepreneur Jaan Tallinn, and its Executive Director, Sean O'hEigeartaigh, was appointed in November 2012. Dr Stuart Russell is an adviser to CESR, along with Stephen Hawking and Max Tegmark. These two organisations investigate a range of other technologies as well as AI.

The newest of the four is the Future of Life Institute, based in Boston. It was established in 2014, and the fact that its five founders include Max Tegmark and Jaan Tallinn illustrates the frequent overlap in personnel between the organisations. It also boasts some Hollywood glamour, with Alan Alda and Morgan Freeman on the advisory board, along with technology entrepreneur Elon Musk, who has donated $10m of his personal money to the institute.

8.6 – Conclusion

We do not yet have a foolproof way to ensure that the first AGI is a Friendly AI. In fact we don't yet know how best to approach the problem. But we have only just begun, and the resources allocated to the problem are small: Nick Bostrom estimated in 2014 that only six people in the world are working full-time on the Friendly AI problem, whereas many thousands of people work full-time on projects that could well contribute to the creation of the first AGI.[50] He argued that this equation needed urgent re-balancing. A very experienced AI researcher told me in spring 2015 that Bostrom's estimate was significantly too low, and that many more AI researchers spend much of their time thinking about Friendly AI as part of their everyday

(50) https://www.youtube.com/watch?v=pywF6Zzsghl&feature=youtu. be&t=45m18s

jobs. Even if that is correct, I suspect Bostrom is still right about the imbalance, and the truth will emerge if we have the kind of debate I argue for in the next, concluding chapter.

Bostrom recently observed that the Friendly AI problem is less difficult than creating the first AGI.[51] We should all hope he is right, as the failure to ensure the first AGI is Friendly could be disastrous, whereas success could usher in a marvellous future.

(51) http://www.ted.com/talks/nick_bostrom_what_happens_when_our_ computers_get_smarter_than_we_are?language=en (15 min 10 sec)

CHAPTER 9
SUMMARY, CONCLUSIONS, RECOMMENDATIONS

We've ventured a long way down the proverbial rabbit hole. It's time to summarise, draw conclusions, and make some recommendations about what to do next.

9.1 – The benefits of disruption

Artificial intelligence is our most powerful technology. It is a young science, dating back only to the middle of the last century, but it has transformed our lives in profound ways, and will do so even more in the future. Smartphones and the value-adding services of the internet are the most obvious manifestations, but AI is involved in almost every organisational process in the developed world, from managing supply chains to allocating resources. The future hasn't turned out the way we expected 25 years ago: it never does. We haven't got hoverboards or jetpacks, but we have got something close to omniscience. With our astonishing adaptability, we have come to take it for granted.

It has been said that the business plans of the next 10,000 startups is simply "take X and add artificial intelligence". There is a huge wave of investment in businesses exploiting AI, and it is enabling new business models that are disrupting established industries at an exhilarating rate – or a terrifying rate, depending where you stand. Pretty much all media industries are being turned upside down, and so are hotels and taxi services. Transportation services generally and healthcare are ripe for disruption, and who knows what 3D printing will do to global manufacturing?

These changes are going to be painful for many, but taken in the aggregate they will improve the quality of products and services and drive down their prices. We will all benefit from that. But it looks very likely that a more extreme disruption will follow within a decade or two.

9.2 – Economic singularity

Automation is the replacement of human work by machines, and it has been going on since the beginnings of the industrial revolution. Initially it was simply mechanisation – the substitution of steam, then electric and oil power for human muscle. This reduced the percentage of Americans employed on farms from 40% of the total workforce in 1900 to 2% in 2000. More recently the machines are showing signs of intelligence. The machines which replaced the ranks of human computers in insurance companies and the armies of secretaries in office buildings everywhere can beat humans at very narrowly defined tasks, like performing arithmetical calculations, and preparing documents.

Throughout all this, the humans replaced by the machines generally found new work, sometimes after re-training. But what happens if, as many people now think, the machines keep getting better at the things we do to earn our income, and there comes a point when the majority of people, through no fault of their own, are simply unable to earn a living? A few decades from now, humans may not be needed to supervise self-driving trucks, buses and taxis. Human surgeons may not be required to check the diagnosis of an AI-powered medical system, and human lawyers may not be needed to interpret the advice of an AI attorney.

The moment when we have to accept that most people will never work again can be described as an economic singularity. If all goes well, the AIs and their robot handmaidens will generate an economy of radical abundance, and humans will no longer be wage slaves. We will all enjoy lives of leisure, keeping fit, having fun with friends, expanding our intellectual faculties. No-one will lack a sense of meaning in their lives. We will find just and fair ways to share the munificence of this plenty, and we will make the transition from here to there without upset.

Well, we can hope. Better still, we can keep an eye out for the approach of this economic transformation, review the different ways to turn it to our advantage, and work out how to avoid the negative scenarios, of which there are many. Many people and organisations are on the look-out for digital disruption and analysing its progress and impact, because it is here and now. There are a handful of organisations sketching the outline of a plan to deal with superintelligence, which we address below, because although it is some decades away at least, it is a potentially existential threat. Curiously, although many people now think that an economic singularity is likely, there is little organised monitoring going on. That is an omission we should fix.

9.3 – Can we create superintelligence, and when?

Our brains are existence proof that ordinary matter organised the right way can generate intelligence and consciousness. They were created by evolution, which is slow, messy and inefficient. It is also un-directed, although non-random. We are now employing the powerful, fast and purposeful method of science to organise different types of matter to achieve the same result. (Although the great majority of AI research is not specifically targeted at creating conscious machines, many of the things it is targeted at will be essential to assemble the first AGI.)

We do not know for sure that the project will be successful, but the arguments that it is impossible are not widely accepted. Much stronger are the arguments that the project will not be successful for centuries, or even thousands of years. However, as we saw in chapter 5, it is at least plausible that AGI will arrive within the lifetime of people alive today. There are plenty of experts on both sides of that debate.

We also do not know for sure that the first AGI will become a superintelligence, or how long that process would take. We saw in chapter 6 there are good reasons to believe that it will happen, and that the time from AGI to superintelligence will be much shorter than the time from here to AGI. Again there is no shortage of proponents on both sides of that debate.

I am neither a neuroscientist nor a computer scientist, and I have no privileged knowledge. But having listened to the arguments and thought about it for a decade and a half, my best guess is that the first AGI will arrive in the second half of this century, in the lifetime of people already born, and that it will become a superintelligence within weeks or months rather than years.

9.4 – Will we like it?

This is the point where we descended into the rabbit hole. If and when the first superintelligence arrives on Earth, humanity's future becomes either wondrous or dreadful. If the superintelligence is well-disposed towards us it may be able to solve all our physical, mental, social and political problems. (Perhaps they would be promptly replaced by new problems, but the situation should still be an enormous improvement on today.) It will advance our technology unimaginably, and who knows, it might even resolve some of the basic philosophical questions such as "what is truth?" and "what is meaning?"

(If you have jumped straight to this concluding chapter, take a deep breath, because the next sentence is going to sound a bit crazy.) Within a few years of the arrival of a "friendly" superintelligence, humans would probably change almost beyond recognition, either uploading their minds into computers and merging with the superintelligence, or enhancing their physical bodies in ways which would make Marvel superheroes jealous.

On the other hand, if the superintelligence is indifferent towards us or hostile, our prospects could be extremely bleak. Extinction would not be the worst possible outcome.

None of the arguments advanced by those who think the arrival of superintelligence will be inevitably good or inevitably bad are convincing. The discussion in chapter 7 concluded that, other things being equal, the probability of negative outcomes is greater than the probability of positive outcomes. That does not mean we would necessarily get a negative outcome: we might get lucky, or a bias towards positive outcomes on this particular issue might be hardwired into the universe for some reason.

What it does mean is that we, as a species, should at least review our options and consider taking some kind of action to influence the outcome.

9.5 – No stopping

We saw in chapter 8 that there are good reasons to believe that we cannot stop the progress of artificial intelligence towards AGI and then superintelligence: "relinquishment" will not work. We cannot discriminate in advance between research that we should stop and research that we should permit, and issuing a blanket ban on any research which might conceivably lead to AGI would cause immense harm – if it could be enforced.

And it almost certainly could not be enforced. The competitive advantage to any company, government or military force of owning a superior AI is too great. Bear in mind too that while the cost of computing power required by cutting-edge AI is huge now, it is shrinking every year. If Moore's Law continues for as long as Intel thinks it will, today's state-of-the-art AI will soon come within the reach of fairly modest laboratories. Even if there was an astonishing display of global collective self-restraint by all the world's governments, armies and corporations, when the technology falls within reach of affluent hobbyists (and a few years later on the desktops of school children) surely all bets are off.

There is a danger that, confronted with the existential threat, individual people and possibly whole cultures may refuse to confront the problem head-on, surrendering instead to despair, or taking refuge in ill-considered rapture. We are unlikely to see this happen on a large scale for some time yet, as the arrival of the first superintelligence is probably a few decades away. But it is something to watch out for, as these reactions are likely to engender highly irrational behaviour. Influential memes and ideologies may spread and take root which call for extreme action – or inaction.

At least one AI researcher has already received death threats.

9.6 – Rather clever mammals

We are an ingenious species, although our range of comparisons is narrow: we know we are the smartest species on this planet, but we don't know how smart we are in a wider galactic or universal setting because we haven't met any of the other intelligent inhabitants yet – if there are any.

The Friendly AI problem is not the first difficult challenge humanity has faced. We have solved many problems which seemed intractable when first encountered, and many of the achievements of our technology that 21st century people take for granted would seem miraculous to people born a few centuries earlier.

We have already survived (so far) one previous existential threat. Ever since the nuclear arsenals of the US and the Soviet Union reached critical mass in the early 1960s we have been living with the possibility that all-out nuclear war might eliminate our species – along with most others.

Most people are aware that the world came close to this annihilation during the Cuban missile crisis in 1962; fewer know that we have also come close to a similar fate another four times since then, in 1979, 1980, 1983 and 1995. [52] In 1962 and 1983 we were saved by individual Soviet military officers who decided not to follow prescribed procedure. Today, while the world hangs on every utterance of Justin Bieber and the Kardashian family, relatively few of us even know the names of Vasili Arkhipov and Stanislav Petrov, two men who quite literally saved the world.

Perhaps this survival illustrates our ingenuity. There was an ingenious logic in the repellent but effective doctrine of mutually assured destruction (MAD). More likely we have simply been lucky.

We have time to rise to the challenge of superintelligence – probably a few decades. However, it would be unwise to rely on that period of grace: a sudden breakthrough in machine learning or cognitive neuroscience could telescope the timing dramatically, and it is worth bearing in mind the powerful effect of exponential growth in the computing resource which underpins AI research and a lot of research in other fields too.

9.7 – It's time to talk

What we need now is a serious, reasoned debate about superintelligence – a debate which avoids the twin perils of complacency and despair.

We do not know for certain that building an AGI is possible, or that it is possible within a few decades rather than within centuries or millennia. We also do not

(52) http://www.pbs.org/wgbh/nova/military/nuclear-false-alarms.html

know for certain that AGI will lead to superintelligence, and we do not know how a superintelligence will be disposed towards us. There is a curious argument doing the rounds which claims that only people actively engaged in artificial intelligence research are entitled to have an opinion about these questions. Some go so far as to suggest that people like Stephen Hawking, Elon Musk and Bill Gates are not qualified to comment. It is certainly worth listening carefully to what experts think, and as is so often the case, they are divided on these questions. In any case, AI is too important a subject for the rest of us to shrug our shoulders and abrogate all involvement.

We have seen that there are good arguments to take seriously the idea that AGI is possible within the lifetimes of people alive today, and that it could represent an existential threat. It would be complacent folly to ignore this problem, or to think that we can simply switch the machine off if it looks like becoming a threat. It would also be Panglossian to believe that a superintelligence will necessarily be beneficial because its greater intelligence will make it more civilised.

Equally, we must avoid falling into despair, felled by the evident difficulty of the Friendly AI challenge. It is a hard problem, but it is one that we can and must solve. We will solve it by applying our best minds to it, backed up by adequate resources. As we saw in the last chapter, Nick Bostrom thinks that just six people are employed full-time on the Friendly AI project. Given the scale of the problem this is a woefully small number, so the establishment of the four existential risk organisations mentioned in the last chapter is an excellent development.

To assign adequate resources to the project and attract the best minds we will need a widespread understanding of its importance, and that will only come if many more people start talking and thinking about superintelligence. After all, if we take the FAI challenge seriously and it turns out that AGI is not possible for centuries, what would we have lost? The investment we need at the moment is not huge. You might think that we should be spending any such money on tackling global poverty or climate change instead. These are of course worthy causes, but their solutions require vastly larger sums, and they are not existential threats.

There is a school of thought which holds that it is too early to have this public discussion. The argument goes that the narrative is too complex to be easily understood by a broad public. Receiving their information through the lenses of time-starved journalists, the public would latch onto the simplest sound-bite, which would inevitably be that the Terminator is coming. This could lead to extremely counter-productive public policy, shutting down labs and companies doing AI research which has nothing to do with AGI, and which should be bringing us the immense benefits we saw in Part One.

Meanwhile, the argument continues, AI research would carry on because (as we have seen) the competitive advantage of wielding better AI than your rivals is too tempting to be foregone by governments, companies and armies. The research would be driven underground (except in authoritarian countries whole rulers can safely ignore public opinion), and as AGI draws close it will be developed without appropriate safeguards.

This school of thought believes that the people who are actually able to do something about the Friendly AI problem – people with world class skills in deep learning and cognitive neuroscience – should be allowed to get on with the job until they can demonstrate some tangible progress. Then a public discussion could be held with more than one simplistic outcome on offer, diluting the risk of damaging policies being hastily implemented.

It is easy to sympathise with this argument: no-one with any sense wants to see AI researchers being vilified and perhaps exposed to attack. But attempts to downplay known or suspected risks are rarely successful for long, and they often result in a backlash when the truth escapes. Furthermore, we need to harness a broader range of skills than excellence in computer science. We may need input from all parts of our giant talent pool of seven billion individuals. Who can forecast what kinds of innovation will be required to address the Friendly AI challenge, or where those innovations will come from?

9.8 – Surviving AI

The title of this book was chosen carefully. If artificial intelligence begets superintelligence it will present humanity with an extraordinary challenge – and we must succeed. The prize for success is a wondrous future, and the penalty for failure (which could be the result of a single false step) may be catastrophe.

Optimism, like pessimism, is a bias, and to be avoided. But summoning the determination to rise to a challenge and succeed is a virtue.

Acknowledgements

This book is an attempt to collect and organise the thoughts of a large number of people. Many of them are mentioned in the text, and suggestions for further reading can be found at www.pandoras-brain.com, which also has information about the fictional counterpart to this book, *Pandora's Brain*, which is available at Amazon and elsewhere as a paperback and an ebook.

Two of the people behind the thoughts and ideas in this book deserve particular mention.

Ray Kurzweil has done more than anyone else to bring the world's attention to the possibility that a superintelligence could arrive on this planet within the lifetimes of people already alive today. He is a controversial figure, not least because of the relentlessly confident and optimistic nature of his predictions.

Reading Kurzweil's book, *The Age of Spiritual Machines* in 1999 was a tremendous eye-opener for me, as for many people around the world, but it left me uneasy. I was persuaded that Kurzweil was drawing our attention to an event of potentially huge importance, but I could not quite surrender to his determinedly upbeat interpretation.

In the years that followed I described Kurzweil's ideas to many people, and I was surprised how few of them shared my perception of their significance. It seemed as if the ideas were hermetically sealed off from the majority culture, which regarded them as eccentric and extreme.

This changed almost overnight in July 2014 when Nick Bostrom published *"Superintelligence"*. Bostrom has brought a powerfully analytical mind to bear on the questions of whether superintelligence will arrive, and if so when, and what the implications will be. His book is the result of many years of intensive thought and research and it is meticulously thorough. It was read by hugely influential characters like Stephen Hawking, Elon Musk and Bill Gates, and when they spoke about it, the world listened. In the last year, awareness that advanced AI brings both immense promise and immense peril has become widespread.

I'm sure that both Kurzweil and Bostrom would freely admit that, like Newton, they saw further than others because they stood on the shoulders of giants – in their cases people like Hans Moravic, Vernor Vinge and Alvin Toffler. There seems little point trying to pin down the exact source of each and every innovative idea our species has had: we can just be grateful that we do have them.

Those of us who have been thinking about these things for years have long felt there needed to be a global debate about the future of artificial intelligence. That has now begun, although we are still in its very early stages.

There is a great deal of mis-understanding in the debate, some of it wilful. Some of what is written on the subject is too academic to appeal to a general audience, and some of it is partisan or fanciful. I have tried to make this book balanced and informative, comprehensive and concise. It is intended for newcomers to the subject as well as for those who are already familiar with a lot of the current thinking about surviving AI.

*

My profoundest thanks go to my partner Julia, who plays the dual role of counsellor and editor with great aplomb. I've also benefited from the somewhat less focused but nevertheless sincere encouragement of our 14 year-old, who is more likely to witness the arrival of the first superintelligence than we are. My hugely talented designer Rachel Lawston has produced a cover which (I think) looks great and answers the brief perfectly.

If it takes a village to raise a child, it takes at least a hamlet to write, edit and produce a book. I am grateful to the following people, who have given their time and energy to support the project, and in many cases to provide constructive criticism on its earlier drafts. All errors, omissions and solecisms are of course my fault, not theirs.

Adam Jolly, Alexander Chace, Aubrey de Grey, Ben Goertzel, Ben Medlock, Brad Feld, Chris Meyer, Clive Pinder, Dan Goodman, Daniel van Leeuwen, David Fitt, David Shukman, David Wood, Henry Whitaker, Hugo de Garis, Jaan Tallinn, James Hughes, Janet

Standen, Jeff Pinsker, Joe Pinsker, John Danaher, Keith Bullock, Kenneth Cukier, Leah Eatwell, Mark Mathias, Peter Fenton O'Creevy, Peter Monk, Russell Buckley, Tess Read, Tim Cross, Tom Aubrey, Tom Hunter, William Charlwood, William Graham.

Have you read . . .

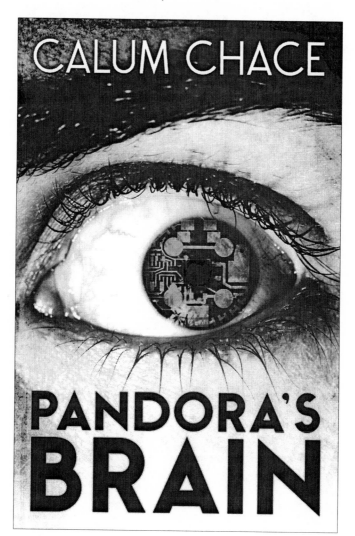

CPSIA information can be obtained at www.ICGtesting.com
Printed in the USA
LVOW08s0809081016

507222LV00003B/210/P